DAFFODILS IN THE BATHTUB

and Other Meditations

RUTH DONKER

CRC Publications
Grand Rapids, Michigan

Library of Congress Cataloging-in-Publication Data
Donker, Ruth, 1923-
    Daffodils in the bathtub and other meditations / Ruth Donker.
      p.   cm.
    ISBN 1-56212-058-1
    1. Faith—Meditations. 2. Christian life—Meditations. I. Title.
BT771.2.D64 1994
242—dc20   94-7277
                                         CIP

10 9 8 7 6 5 4 3 2 1

Acknowledgments

I wish to acknowledge seven friends who read, critiqued, and, in some cases, edited my manuscript. My thanks to Rev. Barry Blankers, Lillian Grissen, A. James Heynen, Rev. Peter Holwerda, Phyllis Ten Elshof, Lorna Van Gilst, and Thea Van Halsema. My daughters Carole Collins and Patricia Pinkis gave valuable suggestions and encouragement, and Sandy De Groot carefully prepared the edited text for submission.

In loving memory of my husband, Luverne, and our son Dan.

Contents

Preface 9

Perspective 10

The View from Above 14

Zucchini and Sin...18

Shortcuts 20

Masks and Facades...22

The Fatal Flaw 24

The Moment of Truth 26

So Much Like Sheep 28

The Heidelbergers Were Right..30

Crossing the Bar...34

Sorrows Like Sea Billows: A Personal Journey.....................................38

There, But for the Grace of God 42

Little Things 46

Behind Closed Doors...50

Faith: How Do You Measure It?..54

Testing, Testing . . . 1, 2, 3 58

The Cross: Foolishness or Power?..62

A Spitting Image..66

Spiritual Suzuki...68

Spiritual Pruning...70

When the Fizz Is Gone 74

In Spite of Everything...78

The One Who Doesn't Change 80

The Tipsy Pigeon...84

It's Mine, All Mine! 88

Holy Huddles...90

The Other Side of the Mountain...92

Joy...96

Go for It! 100

Time to Meditate...104

Remembering...108

Counting the Days...112

Anchors, Storms, Battle Cries, and Shepherds 116

The Great Divide...120

The Greatest Indignity: A Lenten Meditation 124

That's the Life! 128
The Bare Necessities 130
What Is This Thing Called Love? 134
Prescription for Mediocrity 138
God's Gift of Music 142
House Hunting 146
Daffodils in the Bathtub 148
Peter People 152
Corner on the Truth 156
Loosen Up! 160
Like a Little Child 164

Preface

The forty-six spiritual meditations in this collection are unusually personal and wonderfully perceptive. The author speaks from her heart to the heart of the reader, reflecting on her own life experiences and how these have formed and been formed by her faith. She combines a deep sensitivity for all the odd and wonderful things that can happen to us in this life with a powerful faith perspective that has carried her through the darkest days.

Her images and analogies are provocative and striking: sin is like zucchini—it grows out of control; teaching children the basics of Christian faith should be spiritual suzuki, not spiritual boot camp; and church meetings are holy huddles. She tells of a vision she saw at the Heidelberg Castle, portrays the indignity of undergoing an upper G. I. test, and describes music as the fine art that retains a sense of dignity and humanity. She writes of how faith has helped her deal with the sharp pain of losing a husband and a son without losing the perspective "that God does not will evil to befall us."

She writes about life as one who lives by faith and about faith as one who knows in whom she believes.

The author of *Daffodils in the Bathtub and Other Meditations* is Ruth Donker, a free-lance writer who lives in Modesto, California. She is also a news correspondent for *The Banner,* the weekly magazine of the Christian Reformed Church.

Harvey A. Smit
Editor in chief
Education Department
CRC Publications

Perspective

I trust in you, O LORD; I say, "You are my God."
My times are in your hands.
—*Psalm 31:14-15*

A caged bird's only concerns are seed and water—and perhaps escaping a wily cat. Although a bird can see and hear things outside the cage and can sense dark and light, his cage is his world. He doesn't wonder why he's in it or what's outside. Give him food and water, talk to him occasionally, and he's happy. He has no wider perspective.

A baby lives in the present; her constant demands for attention reflect her innocent nature. She does not know that she doesn't *have* to have her bottle immediately, or that crying in the middle of the night interrupts her parents' much-needed sleep. She does not realize that lying in a wet diaper a few minutes longer will not injure her psyche. She wants what she wants when she wants it. She cannot see her needs in the perspective of the needs of others.

Chronic criminals also lack perspective. They have "mental myopia," something we all may suffer from at times. Myopia is a vision defect in which images are focused in front of the eye's retina rather than on it, so that distant objects are blurred. Mental myopia, then, is a deficiency of foresight and discernment. It's like looking through binoculars from the wrong side, seeing only what is right in front of us, not the broader, distant view.

When we live in our own little world, judge others by our feelings and traditions, or view events in our lives strictly in the present tense, we lack perspective.

In periods of grief or sickness, I have sometimes become myopic. It's difficult to bring traumatic experiences and horrible events into perspective—to see the long view, to think five years down the road, to sense the truth of Paul's words to the Roman Christians: that for those who love God, all things work together for good.

Aren't those words hard to believe . . . when a son is killed in the dark of night trying to help someone in trouble? When a spouse suddenly dies and the house mocks its own emptiness? When bills are piled high, cupboards are bare, and children's swollen tummies protrude like ripe watermelons? When a caring woman is denied the gift of motherhood because of a physical problem? When a child is born with deformed limbs? When hundreds die in an earthquake?

Of course they are hard words to believe—but we must make a conscious decision to see such events in perspective. We won't succeed immediately, sometimes not for years, but if we don't eventually view things in perspective, we will live a miserable, dysfunctional life.

Perspective is the capacity to see the relative importance of life's events and to understand the relationship of individual events to the rest of life. When we fight with others over influence and power, over credit for a job completed, or over a theological matter not critical to our salvation, we've lost sight of our place in a needy world and of the redeeming grace of Christ. When grief remains all-consuming, we forget the promise of a new dawn, a joyous reunion, and the reality of heaven. When we forget that there is a time for everything and that God does not will evil to befall us, we've lost the upward look. When we see only the valleys and don't try to climb the mountains, we've lost the larger view. We've lost the ability to rise above ourselves and our situation.

On the other hand, when we hug the mountains and shun the valleys, we are also kidding ourselves. We lack perspective any time we fail to face reality.

Perspective keeps us on an even keel. It helps us sort out the important from the unimportant and handle life accordingly. When we have perspective, we see items such as dry flour, bitter chocolate, salad oil, egg white, yeast, and granulated sugar not individually, but as ingredients which, blended together, will produce a delicious cake.

Perspective helps us see the relationships connecting various events; it helps us watch as God cuts a wide swath through time—with a purpose and control we may not understand yet trust is best.

If we can trust God, believe God's promises, and call him Lord, we can also believe that God is in control, that our times are in God's hands. This perspective gives hope, vision, and a new meaning to life. It means turning our spiritual binoculars around to see the longer view, or looking outward instead of inward.

In his wonderful poem "Rabbi Ben Ezra," the English poet Robert Browning shows what it's like to trust God and see life in perspective:

Grow old along with me!
The best is yet to be,
The last of life, for which the first was made.
Our times are in his hand
Who saith, "A whole I planned,
Youth shows but half; trust God:
see all, nor be afraid!"

Dear Lord, grant me the assurance that my times are in your hands. Give me the faith to know that you always work for my good and the vision to keep a proper perspective through all the events of my life. Amen.

The View from Above

*If I go up to the heavens, you are there; if I make my
bed in the depths, you are there.*
—Psalm 139:8

*When I consider your heavens, the work of your fingers, the
moon and the stars, which you have set in place, what is man
that you are mindful of him . . . ? You made him a little lower
than the heavenly beings.*
—Psalm 8:3-5

Looking down on a small part of the world from high above is humbling, exciting, and comforting. Humbling because we can see how insignificant humans are. Exciting because we get a glimmer of the magnitude of God's view of the world. Comforting because we know God loves us and can easily seek and find us.

My husband loved to fly his small airplane for recreation and contemplation. He always returned to the ground looking relaxed and, in a strange way, otherworldly. I realized why each time I flew with him. From the air, all houses—both mansions and hovels—resembled anthills. Backyard swimming pools—whether blue-tiled Olympic-sized or collapsible plastics—looked like puddles. Cars were insignificant. People looked like specks of dirt. Only the broad patterns of the landscape, such as highways, rivers, lakes, and dams, stood out.

On one of our flights, I remember straining to hear my husband's voice above the roar of the engine as he recited the words of an insightful Persian poet:

> The worldly hope men set their hearts upon
> Turns ashes—or it prospers; and anon,
> Like snow upon the Desert's dusty face,
> Lighting a little hour or two—is gone.

The poet was humbled, and so am I. God must either laugh or cry when he sees us madly accumulating possessions and pompously vying for recognition and importance. It must hurt God deeply to see his image-bearers abuse one another, kill and steal, lie, falsely accuse each other, and laugh in God's holy face.

How puny we are. Who are we that God is even mindful of us? We can never see as God sees, not from an airplane, the Empire State Building, the Eiffel Tower, or the highest mountain. We cannot see the hearts of other people. We do not know how God views the little area we call our world. Nor do we know the big picture. In fact, only by God's grace, providence, and wonderful laws of nature can we fly high above the earth in reverie or stand at the top of a tall building without falling to the ground.

What's exciting, though, is that God sees us as we scurry around taking care of our earthly needs. In God's eyes we are not inanimate specks, but God's own children, just a little lower than the heavenly beings! God numbers the hairs on our heads and knows what we will say before we speak. God knows our sins, our needs, our hurts, and our hang-ups, and looks down not in contempt, but in love.

God lovingly seeks us and will not let go. Francis Thompson's poem "The Hound of Heaven" describes his attempt to escape from God by fleeing into nature and science, intimacy, mysticism, and his own thinking—and his eventual surrender to a God who pursued him relentlessly.

> I fled Him down the nights and down the days;
> I fled Him, down the arches of the years;
> I fled Him, down the labyrinthian ways
> Of my own mind; and in the mist of tears
> I hid from Him, and under running laughter.
> > Up vistaed hopes I sped;
> > And shot, precipitated,
> Adown Titanic glooms of chasmèd fears,
> > From those strong Feet that followed, followed after.
>
> > Still with unhurrying chase,
> > And unperturbèd pace,
> Deliberate speed, majestic instancy,
> > Came on the following Feet,
> > And a Voice above their beat—
> 'Naught shelters thee, who wilt not shelter Me.'

Thompson knew the view from above. He knew God could see his heart. It's good for us to get our own view from above—to be humbled, to get things in perspective. God's view from above leads us beyond humility to see God's majesty, love, and saving grace.

Father, it is comforting to know that even though I may appear as only a speck on the face of the earth, I cannot hide from you. You know me intimately, and you love me. Thank you for the grace with which you claim me as your child.
Amen.

Zucchini and Sin

Direct my footsteps according to your word;
let no sin rule over me.
—Psalm 119:133

Zucchini is one of the enigmas of my life. Who can explain how a small, flat, dead-looking seed tossed into almost any kind of soil can produce so prolifically that rabbits seem sterile by comparison?

Each spring, after I finish the annual housecleaning ritual, my providing and preserving instincts take over—and I plan and plant the vegetable garden. Rhubarb looks fine, I say to myself, but other crops need rotation. Tomatoes here and beans there. No corn this year because the walnut trees interfere too much with the sunlight. Melons over by the asparagus and just a few pepper and cucumber plants. And this year, I tell myself, only two or three zucchini mounds!

I approach the area I've allotted for squash. My packet contains enough seed for six or eight little mounds. I can't waste any seed—not at today's prices—and I can always eliminate plants later when I thin out the seedlings. I make eight mounds, punch holes in them with my index finger, and drop the little time bombs into the eager soil.

From this moment on, the scene runs like a videotape on fast forward. Plants spring up from the ground. Giant yellow blossoms appear, and almost overnight . . . instant zucchini! Early in the morning, the green cylinders may be four inches long, but, growing as fast as Pinnochio's nose, they can be five inches in diameter by nightfall. Even though I yank massive plants from their moorings, the rest settle down more comfortably, stretching their limbs in the newly-acquired space.

We start eating the stuff every night for dinner—but going through zucchini at that rate is like getting rid of a million dollars by spending a dollar a day. In mid-summer, giving becomes obsessive. "Would you like some nice zucchini for supper?" I ask visitors casually, with studied innocence. Most women know two or three zucchini are plenty for a meal, so I address the men, who often fall for the ploy and leave happily with a thirty-pound bag stuffed full.

As the supply and demand ratio spins out of control, I attack the vegetables themselves, wrenching the two-foot monstrosities from their umbilical cords and throwing them in a heap. As the pile grows, my conscience is sensitized. Frugal ancestors—thoroughly imbued with the Puritan work ethic, survivors of the Great Depression or the old country's Great Potato Scourge—haunt my lovely garden and taunt me incessantly, "Waste not, want not!"

The zucchini themselves seem to rise up on their knotted stems, as if on raised elbows, to glare at me, daring me to lay them waste.

In the long reaches of the night, I see squash spilling to my feet from massive machines that cannot be disconnected or decelerated. The dreams turn to nightmares. I am on trial for murder. The judge and jurors are human-sized zucchini. They look on me with ridicule and contempt. They sentence me to eat only squash every meal for the rest of my life.

Sin, it seems to me, is like a runaway zucchini patch. The innocuous seeds we plant in our hearts—or allow to be planted there—appear so harmless. We can handle them. We can use moderation. We won't let them get the best of us.

Maybe initially the sin isn't so bad. Zucchini, too, is good to eat and grow, as long as the growth is controlled. But Satan has a way of taking good things, such as eating, drinking, or sex, and perverting them. We foster the growth of the seeds with all the things sin needs to thrive. Even indifference and neglect won't stop the growth. Soon, what once looked good to us—a lie that could work to our advantage, a deed not wrong in itself—now possesses our lives as the seeds turn to plants and grow out of control. Then, instead of rooting out all of the plants, we let a few keep growing, and they take the place of the ones eliminated. Sin takes over. It haunts us night and day, and the good that was supposed to come from the original planting now condemns us. Only a mediator can overrule the death sentence, root out the evil, and make us free from guilt. That mediator, of course, is Jesus. His solution? Justification by repentance and faith in him. The result? A life free from guilt—free to be all he wants us to be under the care of the great Provider.

*Help me discern the sins in my life, O God, and give me the
determination to root them out. Forgive my transgressions,
cleanse my heart of all impurities, and make me righteous
before you. Amen.*

Shortcuts

*Let us throw off everything that hinders and the sin that
so easily entangles, and let us run with perseverance the
race marked out for us.*
—Hebrews 12:1

When I taught high school English in Michigan some years ago, my department required students in all English classes to read four or five books a semester outside of class. They had to give a written or oral report on each book they read.

During those years, an enterprising publisher was printing a clever aid for lazy students—and was making a handsome profit. Unlike the light-hearted comic books of earlier years or today's space-age comics, these magazines illustrated and condensed literary classics. Why spend hours reading a "boring" 400-page English classic without pictures when you could read the book in modern language and see the action in living color—and in a fraction of the time?

But we teachers were aware of this magazine's existence—and of its penchant for omitting critical parts of a story. We could spot a comic review quite easily, and taking the shortcut often earned a student embarrassment and a penalty.

Sin, I think, is often like those literary comics—a shortcut to the things we want. Lust is a shortcut to real love and commitment; gossip is a shortcut to truth or popularity; robbery is a shortcut to fortune; and cheating is a shortcut to success. Denial is often a shortcut to mercy, and violence cuts corners to justice.

We usually take shortcuts to avoid or abbreviate something we perceive as unpleasant. We cut across a lawn or a vacant lot to avoid confronting a barking dog or taking a long walk. A child denies involvement in a naughty act to escape punishment. People murder to hide evidence of a crime or to avoid having to deal with the victim. Couples use the punishment of silence to avoid a reasoned confrontation or confession.

Shortcuts aren't all bad, though. A cake made from a packaged mix can be as tasty as one made from scratch. Taking the fastest route to a destination can save gasoline and time. Washers and dryers have eliminated a lot of exhausting washboard scrubbing. Building a home with prefabricated walls takes far less time than hammering nails board by board. And a wealth of medical, scientific, and business discoveries have vastly shortened the time and risk involved in many daily procedures.

But so often our shortcuts compromise our principles, impoverish our souls, and weave an incriminating web of deceit and cruelty. In today's text, the writer to the Hebrews talks about the sins that so easily entangle. Often the way out of sin's web is much longer and more painful than the shortcut that led to it.

Maybe instead of taking shortcuts we need to walk the extra mile, offer the other cheek, make a lifelong commitment, tell the truth, put in an honest day's work, confess and repent.

For some people, the "Christian" life is the way of hypocrisy—a shortcut to heaven. With their mouths they declare that they want to serve God. But their actions—or their spiritual inactivity—show they have hitched a ride with the church, looking for a shortcut to the home stretch while expecting the rewards of the faithful. They have adopted the attitude of the sports-car driver whose bumper sticker asked, "How much can I get away with and still go to heaven?"

The only way to God is conversion and faith. The only way to heaven is the hard, narrow way. The only way to true happiness and fulfillment is obedience. The only way to abundant living is by dying to self. The only way to true servanthood is by taking up the cross, not by standing beneath it or walking around it. For all the things in life that truly matter, there is no shortcut.

Lord, I want to live honorably before you. Help me to eliminate hypocrisy and deceit and anything else that would hinder me from taking up the cross in obedience and service to you. Amen.

Masks and Facades

---

*"The LORD does not look at the things man looks at. Man looks
at the outward appearance, but the LORD looks at the heart."*
—*1 Samuel 16:7*

Some years ago, I went for a drive with a doctor friend and his wife after we had dinner together. They went to check on her parents' house, because they were wintering in Florida. When I stepped inside their palatial home, I gasped at its magnificent furniture and decor. Being a book lover, I was drawn to a panel of bookcases covering one wall. Gingerly I touched the gilded book bindings, almost drooling over the collection of classics and other books.

"Pull one out," said the doctor, with a strange smirk on his face. Eager to finger the beautiful volumes, I drew a familiar title from the shelf. To my dismay, I found an empty box, no book. I pulled out another and another. Nothing. Only empty boxes with leather facades.

I had been completely fooled. But so had the owners of the home. They were pretending to be well-read, highly bred, intellectually astute people. But they were as phony as their books. Like a brick facade on a dumpy house, their gold-edged boxes attempted to fill the room with an aura of culture and learning—with something that had eluded them in real life. The owners were equating wealth with culture.

Children are adept at spotting facades. My seven-year-old grandson was riding with his mother down a highway where only the backyards of homes were visible. Many were unkempt, messy, and full of weeds, while the front yards were presumably neat, with mowed lawns and pretty flower beds. "Mom," he asked, "why do the fronts of houses look nice but the backyards look ugly?"

So too with the facades we build and the masks we wear—we want to give a false impression, to conceal or disguise our true selves. Our masks can take many forms—the dirt swept under the rug; the exaggerated personal resume; the charm put on for guests who are long gone when the emotional or physical abuse begins; the prayers that subtly compare ourselves with others; the mortgaged home full of articles far beyond a family's budget; the respected neighbor who rapes women or who regularly steals from his employer.

We can sometimes fool people for a long time. But eventually there is a day of reckoning. The truth comes out, the facade is exposed, the bricks crumble, the resume is found false, the pious prayer rings hollow, the lavish lifestyle leads to bankruptcy, and the lawbreaker goes to jail.

Think about how we must look in God's eyes. Our pretensions do not impress God. God is well aware that Satan hands out masks freely. Some masks may not necessarily be harmful in God's eyes, but neither are they realistic. If, for example, we wear the mask of happiness when we're miserable, we are fooling ourselves, even though we may be seeking to spare others worry and concern.

But other masks are dead wrong. When we wear the mask of temperance to hide the reality of alcoholism; when we wear the mask of respectability and virtue to hide lustful, adulterous, or vengeful activity; when we wear the mask of Christianity while hiding shady business deals, gross dishonesty, gossip, mean-spiritedness, or a love of things more than of God—when we do any of these things, we are concealing, disguising, falsifying our real selves. Then we are not the pure in heart, merciful, meek, poor in spirit, seekers after righteousness, mourners, or peacemakers that God wants us to be.

Excluding the saints who live obviously and indisputably holy lives, I have observed that the more strict, intolerant, ultraconservative, and critical a church member is, the more likely it is that he or she is wearing a mask of piety while hiding some sin. The scandalous lives of some contemporary evangelists, who fervently told others how to live, are painful examples. So are recent revelations about church members—even elders—who have sexually, emotionally, and physically abused spouses, children, and others who trusted them.

Would you agree that we Christians don't like to examine or talk about our motives? We like to believe our motives are honest, pure, and noble. And whenever they aren't, we erect facades to hide them.

When Samuel assumed David's older brother Eliab would be the next king, God told him, "Do not consider his appearance or his height, for I have rejected him. The LORD does not look at the things man looks at. Man looks at the outward appearance, but the LORD looks at the heart."

You know my heart, O Lord, and the motives for all my actions.
Strip my masks and facades, clothe me in your righteousness,
and show me how to live free of pretension. Amen.

The Fatal Flaw

*Yet I am not ashamed, because I know whom I have believed,
and am convinced that he is able to guard what I have
entrusted to him for that day.*
—2 Timothy 1:12

*"I know that my Redeemer lives, and that in the end he will
stand upon the earth. . . . Yet in my flesh I will see God."*
—Job 19:25-26

The scene fascinated me. A snowy-haired ninety-year-old sat tall and straight on the piano bench, in complete control of the sixty-six keys. He wore a tuxedo and white tie. Pinned above his coat pocket was a medal. An internationally renowned virtuoso, he was one of the greatest pianists ever.

His hands were fascinating. Long, gnarled fingers extended firmly from weathered hands marked by protruding deep-purple veins and rounded brown spots. His agile fingers ran effortlessly over the keyboard. He attacked the keys with precision, every entrance perfectly synchronized with the orchestra. His performance was flawless, and he used no music; his brain was a computer with hundreds of floppy discs that contained all the scores he had painstakingly learned throughout his life.

As he played, his face took on an otherworldly appearance, serene and innocent. His eyes looked glazed, as though he should have been in bed hours before. Every crease on his face told stories of the past.

It was during the concert's intermission, when the pianist was interviewed by a television commentator, that his fatal flaw appeared.

The emcee asked a variety of questions—some technical, some philosophical, others personal. When asked about his religious beliefs, the pianist said he was very uncertain about whether a God existed and whether there was a heaven in which he could eventually take up residence.

I felt a sudden, heavy sadness that remained throughout the rest of the concert. Here was a man tremendously endowed with a talent that few possessed and many envied; an old man with his wife still by his side; a man with so much money that he lacked nothing materially. And yet he didn't know whether the God who had created and blessed him even existed, or where he was going after he died.

What was his reason for existence? Perhaps the pianist was basically a sad man with no hope beyond a man-sized hole six feet deep. More likely, however, he felt so much in control of his life that he was not much concerned about the existence of God.

"Trying to get control of our own lives," theologian Lloyd Ogilvie once said, "is like trying to paint our own portrait in a pool of water." It is an exercise in futility. I'm sure William Henley, at his death, found to his dismay that his philosophy—"I am the master of my fate; I am the captain of my soul"—was nonsense, a cruel delusion.

Though many nominal Christians readily embrace the idea that they are home free by cheap grace because all "good" people will go to heaven, true followers of Christ are certain of their place with God forever. Paul and Silas verified the destiny of all true pilgrims when they said, "Believe in the Lord Jesus, and you will be saved" (Acts 16:31). Job, in the midst of all his trials, cried, "I know that my Redeemer lives, and that . . . I will see God" (Job 19:25-26). And Paul, from the depths of persecution, testified, "I know whom I have believed, and am convinced that he is able to guard what I have entrusted to him for that day" (2 Tim. 1:12).

The pianist gave a flawless performance, yet his great flaw was evident when he said, "I don't know; I'm not at all certain." He was like King Agrippa who, in response to Paul's testimony, said he wasn't quite persuaded. Agrippa walked down the dusty road cursed with a self-imposed flaw—the fatal flaw of uncertainty.

Savior, help me to be ready always to witness to the faith I have in you. I claim you as my Savior and Lord. Because of your love and grace, I know I will spend eternity in heaven with you. Amen.

The Moment of Truth

*For God will bring every deed into judgment, including
every hidden thing, whether it is good or evil.*
—Ecclesiastes 12:14

*Jesus said, "If you hold to my teaching, you are really
my disciples. Then you will know the truth, and the
truth will set you free."*
—John 8:31

You may have had the same shopping experience as I. You see a piece
of clothing you'd like to try on. You go to the dressing room, remove some
of your clothing, slip on the garment, and turn excitedly to face the mirror.

Then it happens: the moment of truth. The tiny dressing room suddenly comes alive with mirrors—side view, posterior view, head-to-toe
view. There's no hiding. The garment looks awful on you. It hangs wrong.
It exposes a roll of midriff fat. It bunches up in the back. You double-
check the size and think it can't be right. The garment mocks you as you
take it off, slink out the curtained opening, and disappear.

Or, you're driving along thinking about all the tasks you have to complete before the day ends. You honk impatiently at the car ahead, stop for
a light, and hurry on to your next stop. Then you hear the wail of a siren.
You roll down the window, thinking the officer has made a mistake. You
weren't driving fast. But there it is again: the moment of truth. He says
you were going sixty in a forty-five zone. He clocked you by radar. He
hands you a ticket.

The murder suspect stands before the court. He's confident he'll beat
the rap. He's got an air-tight alibi and a lawyer with a no-lose record. The
suspect leers at the jury as his lawyer wins bout after bout of questioning.
But suddenly the victim's family produces a surprise witness—a man who
could not have known all the details he recites without having been at the
scene of the crime. The dark deed the suspect thought no one had seen
has been exposed to the light of intense scrutiny. The suspect slumps in
his seat. It's the moment of truth: his tangled web of deceit is uncovered.

There will always be moments of truth—when drug user's needle marks show up, when the check forger is caught, when the income tax cheater is arrested, when the secret sin is made public, when the skeleton falls out of the closet.

Yet we all face a more formidable moment of truth when we stand before the law and judgment of God. Everyone who stands before God's law knows they are guilty. All the spiritual mirrors—in which we are supposed to image the Creator—conspire to show us how awful we look, how costly our ticket for disobedience is, how foolish we were to think we could get off scot-free. When we face the demands of the law—and we all must—we face the final moment of truth.

The greatest truth we can ever discover is that God is truth. Jesus tells us that if we obey the commands of God, we will know the truth, and the truth will set us free. Believers can stand in repentance and faith before the cross of Jesus Christ, knowing that when we approach the throne on judgment day, the verdict will be "not guilty."

As a child, I used to fear that on the final day we would have to stand in an interminably long line, in the burning sun (we would, after all, be closer to the sun up there—wherever "up there" is). There would be amplifiers everywhere, and as each person approached the God of justice, her sins would be broadcast for all to hear. I used to shudder at the thought of such embarrassment. This picture haunted me until I realized the magnitude of God's grace and love, the magnitude of God's promise of eternal life to those who repent and believe. That realization, that wonderful moment of truth, brought me peace and joy.

How good it is to know, O God, that for all who love you, the moment of truth—the "not guilty" verdict—has already been revealed. Thank you for the certainty of eternal fellowship with you. Amen.

So Much Like Sheep

We all, like sheep, have gone astray.
—Isaiah 53:6

"My sheep listen to my voice; I know them, and they follow me."
—John 10:27

The twenty-third psalm is a favorite for many people, even those who don't know the Shepherd personally. The psalm is one of many Bible passages that compare humans to sheep.

Although sheep have positive qualities, being compared to them has its down side. We can be grateful that God cares for us, his sheep, but we shouldn't feel overly flattered by the analogy.

Animal breeders say sheep are less intelligent than most other animals. They are characteristically timid, defenseless, docile, helpless, easily influenced, and easily led. They are leaderless and whimsical. They get lost easily. They are so unable to care for themselves that they need a "sheep dip" periodically to be rid of parasitic arthropods. And when sheep are sheared, they stand stoically through the whole process—cold, naked, and dumb.

As a child, the last image I saw each night before climbing the stairs to bed was a large picture of Jesus holding a lamb in his arms. That picture became more meaningful to me after I saw real scenes of sheep in many places.

Once, while traveling through James Herriot's Yorkshire country in England, we had to stop for twenty minutes to let a flock of sheep cross the narrow road. On their way across, the flock wandered, backtracked, and had to be steered by yipping sheepdogs. They had a mob mentality. The sheepherder was almost beside himself getting his stupid animals across the road.

And yet, seeing flocks of sheep covering a rolling hillside is beautiful. I can still picture the daffodil-covered hills near the river Ure in England. Here thousands of lambs cavorted together, some as mincingly as if they'd attended finishing school. The sound of their voices filled the air.

In Middleham, I saw a sheep standing in the cold, nuzzling its dead lamb and bleating softly. One night, from my room in an old country bed-and-breakfast, I heard a sheep crying plaintively and was reminded of the

Christmas song "Listen to the Lambs, All Acrying." In Scotland, on the road between Inverness and Ullapool, large flocks of sheep roamed freely amid the heather and rhododendron, nibbling the grass on the green mountainsides. In the lamb country of eastern Wales, the animals were so well-protected that I was reminded of Bach's "Sheep May Safely Graze."

After having all these experiences, I became more attuned to the similarities between humans and sheep. A lamb is profitable to its owner. Its wool is used for blankets, rugs, and warm clothing. Its skin was used as a cover for the Old Testament tabernacle; it is used today for wallets, diplomas, and other goods. We, like sheep, must be useful to God. We were created to glorify God and to help bring others into the kingdom.

A sheep is a ruminant mammal—one that chews its food over and over. Similarly, a ruminant person takes the time to ponder, contemplate, and meditate. A person's sheepish look shows embarrassment. And sheep demonstrate the meekness we should exhibit.

Pictures of sheep and shepherds run throughout the Bible. An important biblical theme—the sacrifice of lambs—begins early in the Old Testament with the warning to offer no lamb with a defect or blemish. The culmination of this theme is the sacrifice of the Lamb of God, who himself was spotless and perfect.

The prophets spoke often of lost and wandering sheep and predicted that the sheep would be scattered (Zech. 13:7). Jesus characterized people as "helpless, like sheep without a shepherd" (Matt. 9:36). Matthew says God rejoices when one sheep is saved. Jesus himself, who stood dumb as a sheep before its shearer, is the "Lamb of God, who takes away the sin of the world" (John 1:29). He is also portrayed as the Shepherd who feeds his sheep, provides the sheep gate, and searches for the lost lambs.

Yes, we are very much like sheep. We must all admit that we roam from God in various ways. We are defenseless without the Shepherd but safe within the sheep gate. We must be willing to heed the Shepherd's rod, to welcome the comfort of his staff, to be fed in his pastures, to be carried through the dark valleys, to be restored, and to experience his mercy and care.

*You, Lord, are my Shepherd. I need your staff to comfort me
and the prodding of your rod to keep me from straying from
the paths of righteousness. Make me to be your obedient child.
Amen.*

The Heidelbergers Were Right

*Praise be to the God and Father of our Lord Jesus Christ, the
Father of compassion and the God of all comfort.*
—2 *Corinthians 1:3*

In the denomination of which I am a member, one of our statements
of faith is the Heidelberg Catechism. When I was young, children
attended catechism classes weekly, and over the years we memorized the
entire catechism—one hundred fifty questions and answers. We were
grilled question by question. It was heady stuff and surely qualified us all
to be young Reformed theologians. Though I had good teachers, I remember tiring of the year-in, year-out indoctrination, and I had questions about some of the concepts.

Since then, I have found new meaning in this four-hundred-year-old
creed, perhaps because as I've aged, my experiences have verified its
truths. But it also came alive for me after visiting the terraced gardens of
Heidelberg Castle, overlooking the beautiful Neckar River in Germany.

On my first visit, our family was engulfed in one of the heaviest rain-
storms I'd ever experienced. We dashed from tree to tree as we climbed
the cobblestone path to the castle. Illuminated by lightning, the old walls
looked eerie. Thunder crashed around us. Our kids were afraid and
wanted to leave.

The next time I visited the castle, thirteen years later, I had a most
moving experience. I walked through the lovely sunlit gardens with my
husband and another couple on a fresh spring day. Then, by myself, I sat
on a bench and thought about the history surrounding the place.

Somehow, perhaps Spirit-guided, my imagination took over. Suddenly
two young men were walking by, their long coattails blowing in the
breeze, their hands gesturing dramatically. I heard one say, "First we must
talk about our human condition—about sin." "Yes, yes," replied the other,
"but let's not dwell on that too long. Let's talk about salvation. And then,
how to thank God for eternal life."

The two men walked on slowly, sometimes silently, and talked suddenly and rapidly as new ideas came to mind. How to start, they wondered.
What would be the first question? "I have it," one shouted. "Listen:

"What is your only comfort in life and in death?"

There was silence. Slowly the beautiful answer unfolded, phrase by phrase, sentence by sentence, as each added a section. Soon they had poured out their hearts in deep conviction in one of the greatest affirmations of God's love and providence the world has known:

> That I am not my own,
> but belong—
> > body and soul,
> > in life and in death—
> to my faithful Savior Jesus Christ.
> > He has fully paid for all my sins. . . .
> > He also watches over me in such a way
> > that not a hair can fall from my head
> > without the will of my Father in heaven:
> > in fact, all things must work together for my salvation.

I sat spellbound as the two men, hands folded behind their backs, voices growing fainter, walked out of sight.

The touch of my husband's hand on my shoulder jolted me back to reality. It was time to visit the church where Luther had preached and where the Heidelberg Catechism was regularly used.

That catechism, written by Zacharius Ursinus and Caspar Olevianus, was composed at the request of Elector Frederick III, ruler of a German province, the Palatinate, as a "means for instructing the youth and guiding pastors and teachers." It was approved by the Synod of Dort in the early 1600s and soon became one of the most widely published and used catechisms of the post-Reformation period in Europe. It has been translated into dozens of languages.

I still remember most of the questions and answers in the old, unrevised version, and today they have special meaning for me. I love the catechism. I taught it to junior high kids for over twenty years. I'm grateful that, through an excellent denominational education department, the methodology used to teach the catechism has changed. It's been made interesting. It has come to life. Each question is taught not in isolation, but as an answer to a real-life situation. I have experienced the comforting truths of that catechism in both joys and sorrows.

Two months after my experience in the gardens of the Heidelberg Castle, my husband and I were on a business trip more than 1,000 miles from home. At 1:00 A.M. we were roused by the sharp ring of our bedside telephone. It was our older daughter speaking with an urgency we knew meant only one thing—tragedy. Our young son, a paramedic, had been in a medical helicopter accident. There were no survivors. He was twenty-nine years old.

One of my first thoughts came in the form of a flashback. I saw two men walking together in a castle garden. "What is your only comfort in life and in death?" one asked. The other replied, "That I am not my own. . . . That not a hair can fall from my head without the will of my Father."

Father, I confess that I belong to you, body and soul, in life and in death. Thank you for the comfort you provide as you watch over me and work all things together for my good and my salvation. Amen.

Crossing the Bar

Death is the destiny of every man.
—Ecclesiastes 7:2

In my youth, bars—or taverns, as they were called—were considered places of utter iniquity and depravity. We kids were sternly warned, and rightly so, about the evils and terrors of drink. I thought the Lord would strike me dead for even taking a side glance at a bar. That's why I was shocked and confused when a male quartet in our church sang,

> Sunset and evening star,
> And one clear call for me!
> And may there be no moaning of the bar,
> When I put out to sea.

"Why are they singing about bars?" I thought. "Do people in bars moan?" Not until much later did I read Tennyson's poem "Crossing the Bar." The bar was, of course, a nautical term for a sandy obstruction in the water. Tennyson was talking about dying.

Death goes by many names, often by personifications: the Avenger, the Long Sleep, the Grim Reaper, the Rendezvous, the Last Enemy. The rider of the pale horse in Revelation is called Death, and the Bible also mentions the Angel of Death.

Some people cling to life tenaciously, while others long for their last breath. A Bach chorale begins with the words, "Come, sweet death." But the poet John Donne berated death, saying, "Death be not proud . . . death, thou shalt die."

Our attitudes about death differ depending on our life experiences, philosophy, religious background, and spiritual journey toward the life beyond. To some, death is gruesome, mysterious, and best left undiscussed. Children often conjure up monsters and ghosts and creaking coffins. My loving, pragmatic mother, who grew up when adults died in mid-life and children were often lost at birth, wanted us to learn about the realities of life early. Whenever someone from church died, she took us to the funeral parlor. At the local funeral parlor, guard dogs snarled behind a tall fence; the darkness inside the building was so pervasive that I could hardly see the pale corpse; weird shadows played on the wall as visitors huddled by the coffin. I quickly associated funerals with bad headaches caused by trauma and sickeningly aromatic flowers. As I grew older, I avoided funerals.

Some people joke about death and dying. We hear lighthearted talk about "kicking the bucket," "going to that last roundup in the sky," and "throwing in the towel." Someone once wrote,

> Around and around the sun we go;
> The moon goes around the earth.
> We do not die of death;
> We die of vertigo.

Most joking is a cover-up for the fears, questions, and uncertainties people have about death. In the piece "On His Deathbed," Rabelais wrote, "I am going to leap into the dark. Let down the curtain. The farce is over." Some believe that leap is the end of it all. Others speed up the process by shooting themselves or overdosing on drugs. Still others think they will be reincarnated. And a surprising number of non-Christians are certain a good God will welcome them to heaven.

Ministers in my youth often prayed fervently, "Come, Lord Jesus, come quickly." I must admit I often thought, "Why now? What's the big hurry? Christmas is coming. I like school. Give me a break!" But when we pray "Thy kingdom come," we are asking God to usher in the judgment day and the final victory over Satan and death. For the Christian, life on this planet is a preparation for eternal life in heaven. And the older we become, the dimmer the things of earth are, the smaller their hold on us, and the more we desire heaven.

I like the explanation a radio preacher gave when he said, "Death is the comma in the sentence of our life." The best part of that sentence is that it doesn't have a period at the end. We live on forever with Jesus. Romans 6:4 says that we were "buried with him through baptism into death in order that, just as Christ was raised from the dead through the glory of the Father, we too may live a new life."

So we live with our feet planted on this earth but with our eyes looking toward the next life. And we are to leave the time of our home-going to God.

Richard Rogers gave some good advice about anticipating death:

Accustom yourself little by little to die
Before you come to the point that you must die.
He who leaves the world before the world leaves him
Gives death the hand like a welcome messenger,
And departs in peace.

*I know that I must one day die, O Lord. Teach me to
gradually cut my ties with this earth that I may more readily
anticipate the joys of heaven and have no dread of the
uncertainty of death. Amen.*

Sorrows Like Sea Billows: A Personal Journey

"Be still, and know that I am God."
—*Psalm 46:10*

Sorrow comes to us in many forms. Right now I have a lifelong friend who is dying of cancer and grieving that nothing seems to heal her. Another friend sorrows for a grown child who has uprooted her spiritual moorings and has abandoned her marriage, her family, and her God. Yet another friend has an alcoholic husband who won't admit his problem.

In a year's time, hurricanes decimate coastal regions, earthquakes kill thousands, floods sweep victims to their deaths, and brush fires burn homes and acres of trees. In all of these events, people suffer. Grief—over the loss of property, health, possessions, jobs, relatives, and hope—is overwhelming. Sorrow is no respecter of persons; at some time, it strikes us all. I have experienced it too.

I first wrestled with the specter of death when I realized I had no memory of the father I lost when I was four. As a child, I often sat in the large library of our home, the former manse, poring over my father's books and papers for notes that would tell me something about him. The first time I found my name in his handwriting, I was euphoric—yes, I was his daughter! In my teens, I wrote poems and essays about death. I visited my father's grave, wishing I could find him by digging. When my mother joined him thirty-five years later, I mourned a saint whom I felt deserved a special seat in heaven.

My first traumatic struggle with death came in my mid-forties, when my brother died of a brain aneurysm. Since he was just two years older than I, we had been pals all through childhood and had publicly professed our faith together.

When I learned of the aneurysm, I flew to Chicago and found him in a coma. I held his hand—a hand kept warm artificially by machines. I wept when the machines were unplugged. I wept at his funeral. As an older brother led me away from his casket at the cemetery, I raged at God. I shook the gates of heaven.

Back at home, my anger and sorrow turned to depression and illness. I had wrestled like Jacob of old, and I lay spent. I knew my anger was destructive and that I had to develop a sensible philosophy about death. I wanted to make my peace with God.

When, on a moonless night, our son Dan was thrown from a crashing medical helicopter on an unsuccessful rescue mission in the Sierras, I fully experienced the sorrows that roll like sea billows. Yes, I had stages of disbelief and denial, and I asked "Why?" But mostly I experienced the tremendous surges of an uncontainable, uncontrollable sorrow—a sobbing that lasted for hours, retreated, and then, like water crashing against a sea wall, began again with each new wave of grief.

My grief maintained that steady rhythm for months. As I hoed in the garden, my tears splattered steadily on the ground. Driving down the highway one day, I saw three vans just like Dan's blue and white one; I was so overwhelmed with pain that I had to pull over. I once heard a tenor sing "O Danny Boy" and had to flee the auditorium. The billows rolled unabated, night and day. And as I saw others going happily about their business, I wanted to shout for the world's merry-go-round to stop and let me off.

In my dreams, Dan would return and stand before me. I would tell him he had been fatally injured and had to leave. He'd smile and disappear. Over and over he would appear and disappear. When I stretched out my arms to embrace him, they only encircled the air. My husband was equally enmeshed in his own grief; it was hard for us to comfort one another. We could only cling to each other.

Five years later, when my husband was rushed to the hospital, the doctor told me his condition looked grim. Immediately I went to the visitors' chapel to talk with God. In those first moments of panic and shock, I clawed at the mercy seat, grasping for hope. But suddenly the fear was gone, as I left my husband in God's loving hands.

My husband died, and I miss him every day in myriad ways. Sometimes I still reach out in the night and find only an empty pillow beside me. Everything we shared comes back in waves of nostalgia. I thank God daily for wonderful memories and an especially good marriage.

I've learned lessons from my encounters with grief. I no longer argue with God. Mine is not a fatalistic resignation to the misery of death, but a studied choice of how I want to live out my remaining days and a quiet resolve to use painful experiences in a positive way.

Within five years of losing my husband, I lost two more brothers and two nieces. The billows rolled again. Each time I wondered why, but peace came more quickly than in earlier skirmishes with sin and death. A few lines from C. S. Lewis's book *A Grief Observed* carry a message I have found very helpful:

> Just as you can't see anything clearly while your eyes are blurred with tears, . . . and delicious drinks are wasted on a really ravenous thirst, . . . the time when there is nothing at all in your soul except for a cry for help may be just when God can't give it to you; you are like the drowning man who can't be saved because he clutches and grabs.

The Lord says, "Be still, and know that I am God."

When sorrows like sea billows roll, it's wise to be still and remember who rules the world and who said that everything works together for our good if we love the Lord. Even in sorrow, we can repeat the words on my husband's gravestone: "It is well with my soul."

Lord Jesus, you died on a cross for me and suffered more grief than I will ever know. When I sorrow, help me to be still and know that you are God, that you care for me with compassion, understanding, and boundless love. Amen.

There, But for the Grace of God . . .

By the grace of God I am what I am.
—*1 Corinthians 15:9*

Smugness is a sin in which we indulge much more often than we'd like to admit. Some people are smug about their appearance—as though they created their bodies and are on this earth to be admired and envied. The appeal to physical vanity has become a multi-million-dollar business; I wonder how many Christians support it.

Others are smug about material possessions—cars, homes, stock portfolios, clothing, bank accounts, property, jewelry. Some preachers present a gospel of affluence, telling eager listeners that God wants them to be rich. I have heard church members share with their fellowship of believers how thankful they are that they earn a great salary and that their family lacks nothing (materially)—this, when some in the church are out of work, cannot pay bills, and have hurts and needs no one hears about. Is this thankfulness or pietistic smugness?

We can also be smug about our spirituality, our position of leadership in the church, our ease in praying publicly, or our length of time as a believer. We can be smug about our talents, athletic prowess, mental agility, professional accomplishments and degrees, race, ancestry, "faultless" children, and wonderful marriages.

C. S. Lewis, in *The Screwtape Letters*, has much to say about the devil's influence on our smug self-satisfaction. While we talk of God's grace, he says, we act as though our blessings are of our own making.

I have never felt as humbled by my blessings from God as when our family visited the German concentration camp at Dachau. Most of the barracks had been removed, but the high barbed-wire fences, a few dormitories, the gas chambers, and the cremation ovens remained. A memorial chapel had been added. We walked through the camp freely, but even twenty-five years after the war, an eerie pall pervaded the area—as though the wickedness and brutality, the stench of death, and the sorrow of the nations hung low in the German sky.

As we walked, the silence (except for the steady crunch of the gravel beneath our feet) was oppressive. Visitors spoke quietly, the pain of past iniquities showing on their tear-streaked faces. One photo in the visitors' center haunted me for days. In it, a mother, aware that she was headed for the gas chamber, looked down at the three children clutching her skirt. I could almost hear her comforting them with the words, "We're going to take our showers now."

We saw the trenches where the prisoners' blood had been drained from their bodies. We saw the huge ovens where the gassed victims had been piled for burning, and we were told that the amount of fat on a victim's body could be gauged by the color of the belching smoke.

As I looked into the ovens, the thought suddenly came to me—"There, but for the grace of God, go I." It was not on my merit that I stood there that day. It was not because I was better in any way than the thousands who had suffered and died there. Had I been in Germany years earlier, my body might well have been one of those piled in the crematorium.

We left camp toward dusk. No one spoke. No one had an appetite. In no way could we relive the horror experienced by the thousands who died there, but we had seen an ugly, frightening slice of human history.

A few days later, we visited the "Eagle's Nest" in Berchtesgaden, the luxurious bunker Hitler used for protection. While we waited to enter, an American woman and I talked about World War II. I suggested that Hitler had been able to come into power at a time in German history when the people wanted radical change. They were ripe for a dictatorship, though they didn't realize they were pawns in the hand of a madman bent on creating a superpower. "No," she replied matter-of-factly, "it's these German people. They're a warring breed. Always have been. They're all to blame. Americans would never do something like that."

Dissuading her was useless. She was a smug American who did not understand that human depravity is universal and that only by God's grace had she not been a part of that political system gone awry. We all have the seeds of hatred, greed, and violence in our hearts.

When we are proud of how healthy and fit we are, when we look down in horror on "those awful people" gripped in the vice of alcohol or drugs, when we feel that our comfortable lives and successes come from being good people and doing all the right things—we forget that God's common grace covers the whole world, including all our blunders and sins.

And when we are smug about our faith, we forget that we are only sinners saved by grace, who, except for the grace of God, would be looking down into the bottomless pit of hell. Sometimes it takes a Dachau to bring us to our senses.

Your loving care for me, dear Lord, is all of grace, unearned and undeserved. Eliminate pride, smugness, and condescension from my heart and make me always thankful for your grace in saving me from eternal death. Amen.

Little Things

"I tell you the truth, if you have faith as small as a mustard seed, you can say to this mountain, 'Move from here to there' and it will move. Nothing will be impossible for you."
—*Matthew 17:20-21*

Most people know they shouldn't make "mountains out of molehills" or big "to-dos" out of things of minor consequence. Yet, a lot of little things are of great importance to us physically, economically, socially, and spiritually.

Consider holes. A hole in a pocket is a risk to anything we thought was safe there. A hole in a tooth can be costly and painful. A hole in a window lets insects or cold air into a house. A hole in a wall can let a mouse in. And, for sports-minded kids, a hole in a fence is a ticket to a baseball game. Games like golf, pool, Chinese checkers, and basketball all depend on holes.

Nothings can often become major somethings in life. For example, one of my adventuresome grandsons recently choked on a small piece of plastic that had broken off a toy. Outpatient surgery to remove the piece cost his parents several thousand dollars.

The National Aeronautics and Space Administration reported that Atlantis's satellite-on-a-string experiment was ruined by a tiny, one-quarter-inch bolt that jammed the $128 million tether-and-reel assembly.

Little things can be big irritants. You can't walk long with a pebble in your shoe. A tiny cut on your finger can keep you awake at night. The sand in an oyster, a natural irritant, can produce an expensive pearl. A pill that can help the person for whom it was prescribed can do damage to someone else. A nail in a tire can foil your plans for the day. An atom can blow up a city. For me, a dripping faucet or some of Maurice Ravel's music can jangle my nerves immensely.

Small acts of kindness can be big boosters for their recipients. My husband's wink across a room was always a mark of reassurance and love. Have you ever winked at a small, anxious child in a doctor's office? There's an immediate reaction—a smile, a sly grin, a face lit up in a moment's reprieve from fears of needles and probing tongue depressors. When my husband was rushed to a hospital's intensive care unit, two nurses who are members of my church came from other parts of the hospital to ask how they could help. One brought me a glass of water. The other whispered words of encouragement, gave me a hug, and sped back to work. Little things for them. Big acts of kindness to me at a very needy time. Likewise, small acts of unkindness can cause great hurt. We're all familiar with acts like these—and perhaps party to them.

When my older son was a toddler, he came to me one day with his little hands clenched full of camellia buds—the first year my new bush had produced them. "Here, Mommy," he said. "I want you to have all these pretty flowers you've been waiting for." All of those buds would have burst forth in a mass of pink had they been left on the bush. But a little boy, with a heart full of love, let them bloom in my heart instead.

Edmund Spenser, in "Visions of the World's Vanitie," realized the importance of little things. He wrote,

> Hereby, I learned how, not to despise
> Whatever things seem small in common eyes.

The Bible often speaks of little things. Jesus extolled the widow's mite—two copper coins worth nothing in U.S. currency—as a gift worth more than all the money given to the temple treasury. Many of Jesus' parables point out the significance of small things: the harm the little tongue can do; the single sheep that wandered from the flock; the misplaced pearl; faith like a mustard seed. Christ spoke of numbering all the hairs on our head; of his care for a tiny sparrow; of his blessing where just two or three are gathered in his name. He told us to learn wisdom from the ants.

The Bible says small actions can have important consequences. It tells of punishment for those who told little lies; of the sin involved in breaking even one commandment; of the joy in heaven when one sinner repents. Small words are of great significance too. The word *but* makes all the difference in defining our hopes of salvation—"*But* thanks be to God! He gives us the victory" (1 Cor. 15:57); "Whoever believes in him shall not perish *but* have eternal life" (John 3:16); "*But* . . . while we were yet sinners, Christ died for us" (Rom. 5:8), italics added.

When I was much younger, I took the text about faith moving mountains quite literally. With a childlike faith, I ordered the nearby mountains to move. Nothing happened. It wasn't until later in life that I realized I had missed the point—the encouragement and promise from Jesus that even a little faith is valuable, and that through it the kingdom of heaven can expand to world dominion.

Father, make me more aware of the little things I can do for others to make their lives happier. Thank you for the reminder of the mustard seed's potential, and for the little words in the Bible that introduce words of great hope and the promise of salvation. Amen.

Behind Closed Doors

*"Who is this that darkens my counsel with
words without knowledge?"*
—Job 38:2

A few years ago a well-known country singer made popular a song
with the phrase, "And no one knows what goes on behind closed doors."
The sexual overtones were unmistakable as he belted out the refrain again
and again.

Today, a number of physical and emotional experiences that should remain private are shamelessly blared on radios and splashed across television screens. Is nothing private or sacred anymore?

When we hear reports of the rampant sexual, emotional, and physical
abuse—even murder—of children, women, the elderly, and minorities,
we realize that "no one knows what goes on behind closed doors." Too
late the awful truth is exposed to a shocked public.

Military strategy meetings, executive sessions of legislative and religious bodies, high-level business dealings, and underworld planning sessions all go on behind closed doors. They are secretive. No information
can be leaked or the battle might be lost. Someone might be hurt. The
deal might collapse. Thugs might land in jail.

One set of closed doors is far more important than these, however.
They are the majestic doors to the secret counsel of God. God has opened
a door to himself in creation. In nature we see God's creative force at
work. We see the Creator's power, majesty, care, providence, and sense of
beauty and design. We stand in awesome wonder as we sense how small
and dependent we are. How can anyone deny the existence of God?

God has also opened the door in the Scriptures, where the plan of redemption in Jesus Christ is revealed. Jesus saves all who repent and believe. God's will for us has been revealed. Sometimes our confusion stems
from a faulty understanding of the word *will*.

Yet there is much we do not know about God. Much of God's activity
goes on behind closed doors. Before God formed the foundations of the
earth, our Creator and the angels had a planning session. God put the
laws of nature in motion and told the chief fallen angel just how far he
could go—how much he would be allowed to do in his murky, evil world.

We read of closed-door meetings between God and Satan in the fascinating book of Job. Theologians call these workings and decisions God's secret will.

Ironically, sincere Christians sometimes presume that they can push the doors open and discern the great mind of God. When all goes well, they praise God. When something goes wrong, they attribute it to God's will—so God is to blame. They ignore the relentless ploys of the devil; the facts of genetics; the laws of nature, which cannot be broken without ill effects; human responsibility. Unconsciously they make God the author of evil, of humanity's sin, and of the human-induced tragedies in the world.

When my father fell dead of a heart attack just before he was to lead an evening worship service, an elder took my seven-year-old brother to his car and told him to stay there—alone. "God needs your father more than you do," the elder said as he closed the car door on the grief-stricken lad. That elder presumed to know the mind of God, and my brother's resentment of him persisted to his own death.

Well-meaning Christians gave my husband and me a similar explanation when our son was killed. They told of the experience of their daughter—a high school student driving without a license, who left the road, hit a tree, and caused her companion's death. They explained that God had destined their daughter's friend to die that day, and God had used this inexperienced, law-breaking driver as an agent to bring the friend to heaven.

Because God is sovereign, these interpreters of God's secret will tell us, whatever happens—gross negligence, drunkenness, murder, ballot-box stuffing, anger, lying, pilot-error—was planned by God. Whatever happens is God's will. But tell me: doesn't that make us all robots? Doesn't that negate our responsibility for our own actions? Doesn't that make God the perpetrator of sin?

Yes, God is sovereign and has a master plan; but God does not make people sin to accomplish that plan. Otherwise, why would we be accountable to God for our sins?

I don't know why some things happen. I cannot tell why God allows sorrow, death, devastation, severe illness, and horror in our lives and in our world. This is a mystery. This knowledge remains behind God's closed doors. But I do know that the perfect world God made turned sinful because of our disobedience, not because God planned to make us sin. Our Father does not wish ill to befall us, and he is ready and able to turn to our profit whatever happens in our lives. He weeps with us in our troubles.

It is dangerous for people to declare indiscriminately that all events are God's will. Sometimes Satan's will has been done, sometimes our own will. The secret counsel of God remains largely hidden behind closed doors. We second-guess God when we try to listen through the keyhole.

Thank you, Father, for the open doors you have created to yourself and your Son in creation and in Scripture. Guide me to respect the doors you have closed and to know my limitations in discerning your secret will. Amen.

Faith: How Do You Measure It?

*Now faith is being sure of what we hope for and certain of
what we do not see.*
—Hebrews 11:1

*Think of yourself with sober judgment, in accordance with
the measure of faith God has given you.*
—Romans 12:3

The denomination of which I am a member has a custom that is, perhaps, unusual in mainline churches. Two elders regularly visit the home of every member of the congregation assigned to them. In the Dutch tradition, this practice was called *huis bezoek*; we call it family visitation, or home visitation.

I find this a comforting tradition. However, when I was a child, my siblings and I dreaded it. Before each visit, one of my brothers usually set the clocks ahead to hurry the well-meaning elders along. To us, the ordeal was like the Inquisition. There was no small talk. One of the elders read and explained a Bible passage, and then the questioning began—from the oldest down to the youngest. No trivial stuff. No talk about school or personal happiness. As the countdown began and we awaited our turn, we all shrank further and further into our seats.

Always, along with questions about "worldly amusements," came this clincher—"Has your faith grown this year?" I first remember facing this question at ten years old. Had my faith grown? What did that mean? I believed in Jesus Christ as my Savior, and I tried to obey him. But could I put my faith on a scale and weigh it? Could I measure it with a yardstick and chart its growth on the kitchen door? Could I probe it with sonar to monitor the waves it produced?

What could I tell the man, whose eyes seemed to be looking right through me? Though I wanted to ask him what he meant, I knew a simple "Yes" would please him, and he would go on to my younger sister. So that's what I said. "Yes, Mr. Elder, my faith has grown."

Family visitation is more relaxed and enjoyable today, but when I am asked questions about faith, I still wonder what some of them mean. Is faith measurable? In quantity? In quality? Steady, constant, or weak?

Great, small, or insignificant? Dead or alive? Is it like a battery that runs down periodically and needs to be recharged?

Somewhere I read, "Orthodoxy can be learned from others; living faith must be a matter of experience." Augustine made a good distinction between faith and understanding when he said, "Understanding is the reward of faith. Therefore, seek not to understand that thou mayest believe, but believe that thou mayest understand." That's a big distinction. As we seek to grasp intangible verities, we *believe*—no matter what happens. Then with a faith that may falter or grow faint, we seek to understand what has happened or is happening.

Oswald Chambers wrote, "Faith never knows where it is being led, but it loves and knows the one who is leading." That's why I always felt the elders should have asked me whether I had faith in Jesus Christ and was trying to obey and live that faith. Faith must have an object—God. Faith and trust lead to obedience. But the one thing needed first is faith. It's either there or it isn't. It comes as a gift from God as we hear the Word and respond to it (Rom. 10:17).

Yes, faith should mature and become more sanctified, but faith can ebb and flow like the tides. I have known people always strong in the faith who struggled to keep their faith near the end of their life, as they lay year after year in pain. And I've heard young people, untested by life's cruel experiences, who were very sure—cocksure—of Paul's words in Romans 8, "I am convinced that neither death nor life . . . nor any powers . . . nor anything else in all creation, will be able to separate us from the love of God." Life's experiences can grind us down or polish us up, but we often learn the lessons of faith in the shadowy valleys of affliction.

Many texts in the Bible seem to speak of the growth of faith as a process. Jesus told the woman in Matthew 15:28 that she had great faith, but he told his disciples they had so little faith. The apostles asked the Lord to increase their faith, and Jesus prayed for Simon that his faith would not fail. We are told to accept those whose faith is weak (Rom. 14:1). Paul told the church in Corinth, "As your faith continues to grow, our area of activity among you will greatly expand" (2 Cor. 10:15); to the Philippians he spoke of their progress in the faith. And Jesus talked of faith becoming more complete.

Some passages speak about faith as a body of beliefs. We read of wandering from the faith, denying the faith, keeping the faith, being sound in the faith, contending for the faith, having something lacking in the faith, remaining true to the faith, and breaking faith. Grammatically, faith is a noun. But in Old English, faith is a verb. I like that. It's the idea of "faithing it out." Faith is something we work at rather than something we possess and are content with.

All the heroes and heroines of faith listed in Hebrews 11 are commended for their faith, yet verses 39 and 40 say that "none of them received what had been promised. God had planned something better." I had never noticed that text until recently. Of course, we know that they all received God's promises later, or in a different form. But reading the list of names, we can be encouraged that these people were not paragons of virtue with perfect faith. Didn't Sarah laugh when God told her she'd have a child? Didn't Moses get cranky and fed up after decades of slogging through the wilderness? Was Jacob always a man of faith? And David?

In this imperfect world, I know that God forgives us when our faith is weak; understands and loves us when we feel our faith will fail us; strengthens converts in their new, untried faith; and assures us, when we cling to Christ, that our faith has made us whole. No yardsticks. No scales. Just God's arms around us, upholding us as we walk humbly along, weak or strong, trying to be obedient children.

Lord, I believe. Strengthen me when my faith falters and grows dim. Keep me from the doubts and fears that could weaken my resolve to believe. Renew each day the hope that is in me. Amen.

Testing, Testing . . . 1, 2, 3

For you, O God, tested us.
—*Psalm 66:10*

Test me, O LORD, and try me.
—*Psalm 26:2*

A strange theology about the testing of our faith is tripping off the tongues of some sincere evangelicals.

Several versions of the Bible use the word *testing*. The King James Version speaks of the *chastening* hand of God; the New International Version speaks of God *disciplining* his children. All these words indicate that God corrects, purifies, refines, and tries our faith and commitment. But how, when, and why God does this are subject to an interpretation that may lead to the misrepresentation of biblical truths.

Parents discipline their children by correction and guidance. We discipline ourselves by hard work, exercise, self-control, and by purging our noxious sins. The body of believers must be involved in self-examination and reformation. And we are all subject to national and societal laws—and to punishment if we disobey.

Since we are God's children, we also need the discipline and rebuke of our heavenly Father, who is the perfecter of our faith. When we stray or cause others to sin, and when pride prompts us to deny the need for God's controlling hand, we should experience suffering and correction to guide our spiritual development.

Just as someone taps a microphone to test for power and sound, God tests to show us where we are in life—how well we are listening and obeying. God does this more often than we realize, in more subtle ways than we think.

Some Christians always see life's great tragedies as God's chastisement. They tend to look for cause-and-effect relationships in people's experiences. If someone encounters misfortune, these Christians say sin in her life caused God to bring down the heavy gavel upon her. And they find a Bible text to prove it.

I am a sinful person. I need the hand of the Lord to guide and redirect my life. But I do not believe that God one day decided to test me because he thought my family needed a king-sized shake-up. I don't believe God caused a motorist in the mountains to fall asleep at the wheel, resulting in an accident and the need for an air ambulance; and that God then sent a pilot, a nurse, and a paramedic (my son) in a medical helicopter to rescue the patient on a moonless night. Or that God caused the inexperienced pilot to become spatially disoriented and to crash into a tree, throwing the other two rescuers out of the vehicle onto the ground, while the pilot burned to death—leaving three extended families and whole communities grieving for years.

Did God cause all this to say to us, "Now, are you going to be better Christians and have more faith?"

Some people would say, "Yes, that's what God did, to mold you after his will." Or they would say that maybe God wanted to discipline one of the others in that helicopter and our son was the innocent victim of God's lesson for the day, like a whole class staying in for recess because one kid was naughty.

For me the scenario plays out differently: a highway accident occurred, and the pilot should have canceled the rescue flight when he felt he couldn't make it to the scene. God is in control of all things, including the laws for living safely and the laws of nature. In this case, God's law of gravity was defied.

We seem to have a paradox here: God controls all things but doesn't cause all things. Sometimes the devil causes our misfortunes, and sometimes we cause them by our own disobedience or stupidity. We may never blame God for our sins, our errors of judgment, or our lack of common sense. Nor can we claim to be robots helplessly manipulated by an avenger who gives us no choice.

After that accident, God lovingly took care of us and helped restore our broken hearts. God strengthened our family, church, and community and reminded us all of the brevity of life. God cried with us and used the tragedy for our good and his glory. God is not a spiteful sadist, zapping people willy-nilly to show power.

Yet well-meaning Christians quote Scripture, saying, "The Lord disciplines those he loves" (Prov. 3:12). Then they worry because they aren't being put through the refiner's fire. "Doesn't God love me?" they ask.

After our son's death, we were told by several people that God must have loved us tremendously to take our son from us. I agree that the Father loves us much, as he loves all his children, but by this reasoning I am led to ask, "Couldn't he have shown his love in a gentler, less violent way? Are we supposed to want still more so he can show us even more love?"

These simple, cause-and-effect theologies about testing cannot be correct. God does test us in numerous ways—and teaches us important lessons in the process. But our Father is not vengeful. We are precious in his sight. He does not make people sin to accomplish his purposes.

Nor is faith necessarily strengthened through trying experiences. I have dear friends who said that a child's or spouse's death seriously weakened their faith for a while. C. S. Lewis in *A Grief Observed* and Sheldon Vanauken in *A Severe Mercy* both describe similar experiences. Eventually, both came to see that God was with them in their grief—but not the cause of it. That's a significant difference.

L. Thomas Holdcroft has said, "God isn't so concerned with delivering us out of the mess we're in as he is in seeing we grow out of the mess we are."

That, I think, is the proper focus. A sovereign God, who gives us choices in all areas of our lives, sometimes allows unpleasant events to occur in our lives, even though we may have to bear the consequences. God refines and sanctifies us so we'll eventually feel right at home in heaven.

Father in heaven, I know you are a good God and you do not cause me to sin. In your providence you allow experiences in my life which I would not choose, but I trust you to use them for your glory and for my eternal good. Amen.

The Cross: Foolishness or Power?

"Anyone who does not take his cross and follow me is not worthy of me."
—Matthew 10:38

For Christ did not send me to baptize, but to preach the gospel—not with words of human wisdom, lest the cross of Christ be emptied of its power. For the message of the cross is foolishness to those who are perishing, but to us who are being saved it is the power of God.
—1 Corinthians 1:17-18

A cross is defined as a gibbet, usually of wood or metal, in one of three forms—an X, a T, or a †. A cross means different things to different people. Various cross forms include the Latin, the Greek, St. Andrew's, the Tau, and the Celtic (or Ionic). The Maltese and the Swastika are more complicated cross forms. The crucifix is a cross with the figure of Jesus on it, often used by Roman Catholics.

Crosses are displayed in churches, placed on tombstones, worn as jewelry, and sung about in hymns. But what does the cross mean? Of what is it symbolic?

In grade school I had to memorize a poem that made me sad. It read:

> In Flander's fields the poppies blow
> Below the crosses, row on row,
> That mark our place, and in the sky
> The larks, still bravely singing, fly
> Scarce heard amid the guns below.

I've seen that field in Flanders—and many other military cemeteries throughout the world. Always, I have felt a deep melancholy viewing row on row of white marble crosses—as well as Jewish stars of David—stretching out neatly across the green grass, seemingly to infinity. Near Normandy Beach on the rugged coast of France, nine thousand young men are buried. Fifteen thousand were shipped home to the United States for burial. In a German cemetery outside Abbeville, France, twenty-two thousand Germans lie, six deep, under weathered gray crosses. And in Epinal, on land donated by the French, fifty-two hundred American men rest where the air is sweet from roses planted at each cross-marked grave.

The list goes on. At the American Cemetery in Cambridge, England, thirty-five hundred are buried. A wall lists the names of five thousand more who were missing in action. In the chapel a plaque reads,

> In proud and grateful memory of those men of the United States Army and Air Force who from these friendly shores flew their final flight and went to meet their God. . . . Into Thy hand, O Lord.

They lie in Arlington National Cemetery, in the San Francisco Presidio, in Manila, in valleys of death all over the world. Thousands lie with crosses marking their graves. What do these crosses symbolize? Were all those young servicemen Christians? Or do the crosses romanticize these death fields and make commitment to country synonymous with commitment to Christ?

In Roman times, death on a cross was a common punishment and a mark of infamy. Throughout history, pain and affliction have been labeled "crosses." The practice of making the sign of the cross, which started about 200 A.D., was often considered powerful. Constantine went into battle with the sign of the cross and won. The cross was also the symbol of the Teutonic knights and eventually led to heraldry.

Does the cross symbolize the sacrifice of a life, an indefinable spiritual force, a mark of loyalty, a commitment to some kind of victory? Is the cross a badge of courage?

In Matthew 10:38, Jesus calls his followers to take up the cross and follow him, and Paul in Galatians 6:14 says that he boasts in the cross. Here the cross symbolizes Christ's sacrifice for our sins. It marks his victory over the powers of evil.

One Good Friday in Manila, I saw barebacked Filipino men lashing themselves with long whips till their bodies were bloodied and battered. I saw others dragging heavy crosses to atone for their sins. One man was nailed to a cross in an annual attempt to be cleansed of evil.

Unlike these reenactments, Christ's death on a cross was a one-time event. It is past tense—finished. No cross we bear can compare to his sacrifice. Any cross we take up must be carried out of commitment to Christ and his kingdom.

Crosses in cemeteries may symbolize commitment to Christ, but for many they are simply a mark of valor and a symbol of dedication to country. Although we can be thankful for the sacrifice of those who died for our freedom, unless they were committed to Christ, crosses on their graves are foolishness.

The cross, said Paul, is the power of God. We don't sit under it, or walk around it, or worship it. We carry its message—the message of what happened on it—to a dying world.

Thomas à Kempis said, "Carry the cross patiently with perfect submission, and in the end, it will carry you." The theologian Charles Spurgeon advised, "There are no crown-wearers in heaven who were not cross-bearers below."

The cross is foolishness to those who do not believe. It may mean persecution and death for those committed to Christ. It is always, as Paul said, the power of God. Consider it carefully. Carry it willingly. Wear it humbly. And look to the day it becomes a crown.

Lord, the cross on which you died is not foolishness to me, but a symbol of your sacrificial love and faithfulness. May its message empower me to help others to find in you their strength and salvation. Amen.

A Spitting Image

*For those God foreknew he also predestined to be
conformed to the likeness of his Son.*
—Romans 8:29

At California's Yosemite National Park, one of the main attractions used to be a placid body of water called Mirror Lake. I have old pictures of those quiet reflecting waters. If you turn the pictures upside down, the lake looks the same as it did right-side up. The mountains surrounding the lake were mirrored so perfectly in the still water that their "spitting image" was formed. Visitors were always silenced by the beauty of the phenomenon. Unfortunately, Mirror Lake has since gone the way of most mountain lakes in their continuing evolvement.

The phrase "spitting image" may be a coarse intrusion in a discussion on natural beauty. The expression seems to come from the practice of using saliva to clean or polish something, as parents do almost unconsciously with grubby little faces. It communicates the idea of making someone as exact an image or reflection of someone else as possible.

I taught junior high students in school and church for years and was amazed each year as the new class entered the room. It was never difficult to tell whose child each one was; some were almost clones of their parents. One girl had the shy, flirty eyes of her mother. One boy seemed as opinionated and dogmatic as his father and even gestured in the same way. The sweet, innocent look, the whiny voice and perpetual frown, the winning smile and amused reactions, the handwriting—all were evidence of a child's daily patterning after traits of his or her parents. The same held true for many adopted children.

A sculptor carving a dog out of a block of wood was asked by an amazed bystander how he could so perfectly create the animal's features. The artist replied, "I just chip away everything that isn't a dog."

Christians are called to conform to the likeness of Christ, to look like Christ, to act like Christ, and to talk like Christ. We're to imitate him in every way. Others should be able to see Christ in us. After all, we were made in his image and adopted as his spiritual children.

How can we image him while the rusty nails of his cross still rattle in our pockets? When we have not sought forgiveness? When the natural inclination of the heart is sinful and selfish? When we constantly battle our sinful innate tendencies, our flawed characters? When we live secret lives that sharply contrast our public lives?

Pious talk doesn't cut it with God. God sees through a pretense of spirituality and is insulted by our hypocrisy. God hears the nasty things we say about others and sees the seedy stuff we watch on TV and the manipulative way we get our personal agenda enacted. God looks into our hearts, sees the spiritual arteries blocked by clots of evil, and knows our urgent need for a heart transplant. So often, God doesn't see himself in us at all. He sees only measly counterfeits.

So how can we be the spitting image of God? By letting the master artist chip away everything that is not Christ. The process may hurt terribly. When it's over and we are taken to heaven, we may not look much like our former selves. God will have to help us recover and refine our holy resolve. We'll have to quit being impressed with ourselves and resolve to be like God. We'll need to do a lot of pruning and praying. Since our mirror is cracked, we cannot see to change ourselves. Only when we abandon our independence and surrender to the one who can restore fallen images, do we begin to mirror God.

Then we won't be concerned about being considered successful, smart, wealthy, and influential. We will want to be known as the spitting image—in appearance, speech, and actions—of Jesus Christ. Not an impostor who gives the Judas kiss, but a person so filled with the Spirit of God that the priority of our lives is to do God's will, amply revealed to us in his love letter, the Bible.

Chip away everything in me that is not Christ, dear Lord, and make me more clearly image you in all I think, say, and do. Unclog my spiritual arteries and allow my love for you to flow freely in every activity in my life. Amen.

Spiritual Suzuki

Train a child in the way he should go, and when he is old he
will not turn from it.
—Proverbs 22:6

Once, driving down a city boulevard, I heard a radio playing so loud that the steady bass beat hurt my ears. Although the sound seemed to come from all directions, I discovered its source when traffic stopped for a red light.

It was the car ahead of me. All its windows were open, and behind the wheel sat a shirtless young man with unkempt hair. He jerked his body wildly to the rhythm of the music. He spit out of the window and drew his fingers through his hair. Impatiently he revved the engine and spit again. His bumper sticker read, "Heaven doesn't want me, and hell's afraid I'll take over."

It was difficult not to label this young image bearer of God a punk. But I had to give him the benefit of a doubt, for in his own crude way he acknowledged a heaven and a hell. Maybe he was a rebellious kid from a Christian home. Perhaps he had problems far greater than I'd ever experienced. Maybe he needed a good dose of love and care. Maybe a weeping mother was bent over a half-empty cup of coffee at that moment, praying for her son. And just maybe he and I will be gazing at the Lord together in the heaven he thought didn't want him. No need to judge or speculate.

In spite of exceptions to the rule expressed in Proverbs 22:6, the wise words of this text ring true in the lives of our children. We reap what we sow. How fertile a young mind is, how full of questions about God, death, origins, heaven, right and wrong. And how quickly evidences of sin appear in that young life.

Just watch children interacting in a nursery, even a "Christian" one. They hit and pinch, slap each other's heads, snatch toys from one another, and test the caretaker's disciplinary resolve. Little ones are not always angels, eager to do good, devoted to others rather than self. Watch how stubbornness turns to a tantrum. Listen to the screams of defiance. It's not the environment or others' naughty examples that cause children the most trouble. It is their own willful nature.

In the life of a Christian child, basic training must start early. The Israelites, who did not have the written Word as we do today, were told by

God to instruct their children constantly—when they awoke, when they went to bed, in "their down-sittings and their uprisings." Train them to be God's children. Teach them to obey. Help them to be his witnesses. Familiarize them with their heritage, their covenant with God. The trip to the land of Canaan might not have taken forty years if there had been consistent training in obedience.

In the military, training takes place in boot camp, where lessons are vigorous, exhausting, and often punitive. Training begins with a nasty haircut and painful shots to prevent diseases. Trainees soon learn to obey orders, to defend themselves, to use and care for equipment, and to be competent soldiers. I knew men during World War II who were sent to Normandy after only six or eight weeks of training. They had been given the basics, and their lives depended on how well they practiced them. Many never had a chance to test the basics; the enemy mowed them down from protected attack areas.

A "spiritual boot camp" is too severe a method of indoctrinating children. The basics of the Christian faith should be taught in a pleasant way so children can hear them, live them, learn the virtues of walking with God, and practice what they have learned. That kind of learning can be fun.

Several of my grandchildren are learning to play the violin by the Suzuki method. Rather than learning notes, scales, keys, and signatures before playing a piece, children learn by playing. By playing simple songs like "Twinkle, Twinkle, Little Star," they learn fingering, rhythmic patterns, bowing, and posture. Suzuki training is not cumbersome, overly-demanding, or unpalatable. Students learn the basics through an enjoyable teaching method. What remains is practice, always following the basic rules.

Our children need a well-developed, practical "spiritual Suzuki." Parents, school teachers, and the church must work together to train children in the way they should go—without discouraging them through our teaching methods. If we do our part, we can leave the rest to a loving Father who always keeps his promises.

Lord, I learned the basics of the faith many years ago, but sometimes I fail to practice them. Help me to be diligent in applying the teachings of the Bible to the way I live and in showing others the enjoyment of learning about you and living the Christian life. Amen.

Spiritual Pruning

"If your hand or your foot causes you to sin, cut it off."
—*Matthew 18:8*

*"I am the true vine, and my Father is the gardener. He cuts
off every branch in me that bears no fruit, while every branch
that does bear fruit he prunes so that it will be even
more fruitful."*
—*John 15:1-2*

It was January in California, the time to prune rose bushes—all eighty-five of them. Dressed in a long-sleeved shirt and armed with leather gloves and pruning shears, I faced the challenge.

The Floribunda and tea roses were huge, most of them about five feet tall with long, intertwining stems and suckers. The leaves were still on the plants, so it was difficult to appraise what needed to be lopped off. But by cutting out the dead wood and the overgrown centers, I could stand back and decide what else had to go.

Some bushes were harder to prune than others. But I knew that the more severely I pruned, the sturdier the plants and more abundant the blooms would be.

As I finished each bush, I felt a sense of satisfaction. True, the bushes looked shorn and stubby, standing eighteen inches off the ground; but there was beauty in the design—like a leafless tree silhouetted against the sky at dusk. The plants looked much better pruned than they did overgrown and drooping with flowers, whose lives had ended somewhere between bud and full bloom.

Pruned bushes and trees have an artistry all their own. In the early spring in California, you can ride for miles past neat rows of trellised vineyards, their vines symmetrically arranged along the wire guides. So too with fruit and nut trees—and roses. Fertilizing and spraying would come later. For now it was enough to see them nourished by abundant winter rains, protected by a dormant spray, and looking the way rose bushes were meant to look at this stage in their cycle.

So much like life, I thought. And in that moment, feeling good about my pruning, I wondered whether God has the same reaction after working in our lives to make us what we are meant to be; after helping us get rid of the scruffy, superfluous baggage we tote around—our unproductive dead wood, our overgrown center, and our wayward untrained growths.

God is the master gardener. God is a pro at shaping us according to a perfect plan for his glory and our best interest. God does not prune recklessly but has perfect judgment and divine accuracy. God does not cause the problems in our lives—our sorrows, temptations, sins, and bad decisions—but God does use them to make us more disciplined, fruitful branches of the perfect vine, Jesus Christ.

Many areas of life require some sort of pruning. How many blueprints do engineers toss aside as they change calculations, eliminate structural weaknesses, and view a plan from all angles? Or how many notes do composers delete or change before they are satisfied with a musical composition? One composer said it is easy to compose, but it is wonderfully hard to let the superfluous notes fall under the table.

At a journalism workshop I attended a few years ago, the leader gave a rather severe formula for good, succinct newswriting. He said that when an article was completed, we should go back and delete half the words, including our prized words—the cutesy phrases, high-sounding terms, subjective adjectives. Why? Because a news writer is delivering facts. Her views about the facts are unimportant. Readers don't want an essay. They want the news.

All journalists have to prune their writing, discard words by the pagefull, and search for the most precise way to express facts and ideas. And still the editors will swoop down with red pens and finish the job.

We also "prune" our bodies. Think what our bodies endure as we try to keep them in shape: we cut hair, blow noses, pull teeth, amputate limbs, clip fingernails, cauterize warts, reduce fat, remove gallstones and appendixes, and excise tumors. We follow "how to" books meticulously, but there is always room for improvement.

The Scotch poet Robert Burns perceived an important truth when he said, "O wad some Pow'r the giftie gie us/To see oursels as others see us." We don't usually see ourselves—our sins and bad character traits—as well as others do. It's sometimes helpful to see ourselves as others see us, but it's far more important to see ourselves as God sees us.

Burns's "some power" is, of course, God. And God has written a guidebook for self-examination and pruning. It's not difficult to read, nor is it written for people free of fault and in perfect alignment with the vine. It is written for sinners who can be transformed into saints. In the guidebook, God tells us what is expected of us, what we should get rid of, and how we should live. Self-pruning can be deflating. When done correctly, however, it is like the self-examination we should perform before we partake of the Lord's Supper.

We need to be diligent and amenable as we follow the divine guidebook, as we ask God to help us eliminate sinful thoughts, character flaws, and hidden sins, and as we slowly become fruit worthy of the Gardener.

Prune me, O Father, and cut away all that is detrimental to my spiritual growth. May I bear fruit worthy of you, the master gardener. Amen.

When the Fizz Is Gone

*"I know your deeds, that you are neither cold nor hot. I wish
you were either one or the other! So, because you are
lukewarm—neither hot nor cold—I am about to spit
you out of my mouth."*
—Revelation 3:15

An advertising jingle that the producers of Alka-Seltzer used to use
goes like this:

Plop, plop, fizz, fizz—
Oh, what a relief it is.

The song seemed to be good advertising, because it appealed to the
senses. You could hear the tablet plop into the water and watch it fizz as it
quickly dissolved. A consumer, holding his distressed stomach, grabbed
the glass and emptied it. A look of serenity followed. The tablet and relief
became synonymous—you take the right stuff, and there are results. Life
is good again.

But did you ever reach for a tablet from a shelf-worn carton, plop it
into a glass of water, and see it fall to the bottom? A dud. No fizz. No relief. Only a non-effervescent, tasteless liquid, as ineffective as a car with a
dead battery.

Alka-Seltzer is supposed to fizz and relieve indigestion. A cup of coffee is supposed to provide comfort and warmth and get the adrenalin
moving. A lamp is supposed to produce light. Salt is supposed to enhance
the taste of food and be both a preservative and a cathartic.

Life is meant to be interesting, full, and enjoyed daily. Marriage is
meant to be filled with love, commitment, and joy. Friendships are meant
to be enriching, mutually beneficial, and companionable. And the Christian life is meant to be an abundant, growing, sanctifying experience full
of God's grace and love, mercy and forgiveness, and peace—a life in
which we share the good news of salvation and live thankfully.

Yet many events and experiences conspire to take the fizz out of living.
Sometimes these experiences are self-imposed. But everyone who has
gone through dark valleys knows it is hard to pray when tragedy strikes.
Deep depression can make us listless and estranged from God. The ener-

vating effects of prolonged illness can blunt spiritual vitality and vigor. An unfaithful friend or spouse can leave us humiliated, empty, and joyless. Sometimes life can seem like such a "bum deal" that thoughts of suicide surface.

Life can become a drag, a dull routine of mundane, repetitive, meaningless happenings. The pizzazz goes out of marriage. The blush of romantic love turns to rejection and cruelty. Excitement sours to revulsion. Partners take one another for granted like old, muddy garden boots. Love and marriage are no longer synonymous. The fizz is gone.

The Christian life, too, can become lukewarm, as tepid as a warmed-over bowl of stew. Worshipers sit unsmiling in church, pop candy to relieve the boredom, sing halfheartedly, critically clock the sermon, and leave unchanged, unaffected by the holy presence of God. Some who claim to wear the cross on their foreheads do nothing inside or outside the church to serve others. They are solemn, unbending, uncooperative, and spiritually withered. They're like the wealthy Laodiceans. They've lost their first love. As the footnote in my Bible puts it, they are supplying "neither healing for the spiritually sick nor refreshment for the spiritually weary."

Think back on your first love—soaring on a swing; eating an ice cream cone; winning a competitive game; enjoying pizza parties, pajama parties, or trips to the big city; the great outdoors; your work.

Think back on your courting days—the stars in your eyes, vows of undying love, listening to "your song" together, heartache when you were apart. Those were heady days. Beautiful, dream-filled days.

Think back on your first commitment to Christ—the joy of finding him and becoming a part of his family, the desire to shout his good news from the housetops. You volunteered to teach, to witness, to work hard in the church. You prayed often and fervently. You couldn't say enough about Christ's love for you and your love for him.

Is the fizz gone? To some of these scenes we can never return. They are gone. Life has moved on. Your spouse has died. You can't eat pizza anymore. The only pajama party you can have is in your sickbed. You don't have many Christian friends left. Swings scare you and ice cream gives you a headache. You're out of work. Life has thrown you a curveball.

Now take inventory. Has God ever copped out on a single promise he made you? Have you become too critical of your spouse or friend or church? Are you making excuses to avoid kingdom work? Do you feel entitled to slack off because you've done your share?

Unlike seltzers or cola, the fizz can come back into your life. A first love can be renewed. Spiritual commitment can return—maybe in a deep, abiding peace through divine forgiveness; maybe after introspection which leads to renewed interest and participation; maybe in a spiritual Alka-Seltzer that relieves your disappointments, lethargy, and upset soul.

Joy in life, in others, and in Christ can come back to stay. Ask God to bring back the fizz—that first love, that fresh start. Then start living again.

Lord, make my life in Christ all it was meant to be. Remove my lethargy. Renew my commitment and love for you, energize me with your Spirit, and fill me with a holy resolve to be a joyful Christian, dedicated to wholehearted service.
Amen.

In Spite of Everything

I can do everything through him who gives me strength.
—Philippians 4:13

People who get things done when the odds are against them always inspire me. They have the kind of grit and determination that defies obstacles, challenges every ounce of energy, and leaves the skeptical onlooker with mouth agape.

Dvořák, the foremost composer of Bohemia, was not born a privileged member of society. His musical talents were obvious early in life, but he had no money to pursue an education. As a young person, he was said to have had a thousand tunes running through his head, but no piano to help him compose and no music paper on which to record his ideas. A weaker man might have given up and bemoaned his fate. But in spite of his difficulties, Dvořák composed the much-loved Symphony in E Minor (*From The New World*) and other works, led orchestras, and became appreciated around the world.

In a Manila ghetto, I was amazed to see hordes of little children wearing the whitest T-shirts I've ever seen. Mothers wash the clothes in polluted streams and hang them out in the sun to dry. The same children, when given gum or candy, always said a polite "thank you." They may have been living in hovels made of cardboard and tin, but their mothers had enough self-respect and inner drive to dress them in clean clothes and teach them respect and common courtesy.

Examples abound of people who—though almost everything is going against them—are living productive, fulfilling lives. Rather than mope, they are determined to make something of themselves and influence others.

A man blind from birth becomes minister of a large church. A paraplegic hikes to the top of Half Dome in Yosemite National Park. Joni Eareckson Tada, paralyzed in a swimming accident, lectures, sings, writes using a pencil in her mouth, and gives radiant testimony to God's grace in her life. A criminal serves out his sentence for a horrible crime, turns his life around, and dedicates his life to prison ministry. A mother, lying every day in an iron lung, inspires her family by her calm faith in God. A poor child, living in the slums, struggles to get an education and becomes a college president. All of this . . . in spite of everything.

Our text says, "I can do everything through him who gives me strength." Of course, some people rise above seemingly insurmountable circumstances without acknowledging divine help. Yet, whether they confess it or not, they are given their strength by God.

"I can do everything" or "all things"—I've often pondered what is included in these words. A footnote in my Bible defines *everything* as "Everything pleasing to God," Christ being the source of Paul's abiding strength. The second half of 2 Corinthians 11 records the tremendous number of difficulties Paul faced and how he endured them in spite of everything and everyone working against him.

For the Christian, power and strength are assured. We can triumph over tragedies, heartaches, sickness, loneliness, and persecution in the strength God gives to us through Christ. One author wrote, "He who fears God need fear nothing else, and he who fears not God needs to fear everything else." God gives us strength in our weakness and frees us from fear.

In my younger years, I said that if I lost my husband or any of my children I would not be able to go on living. Yet I lost a child and a husband within five years' time, and I'm going on. It can be done. I was short-changing God and limiting his abilities. I still grieve my loss; that never goes away. But at the same time I can move ahead triumphantly—in spite of everything.

Consider this story. A small team of church planters plugged along with a nucleus of only ten or twenty people. With faith in God, they made plans for a church building and for several church programs. Had they asked a business consultant for advice, they would have been told there was no chance for success. Yet, two years later, that valiant group had grown so large it began to form a daughter church.

In our endeavors, we may not tempt God, try to manipulate God to do our will, or be grossly unrealistic or reckless. But with God's strength and through faith, we can rise up like eagles and do things others think impossible. In spite of everything.

Heavenly Father, teach me to rise above difficult and
seemingly impossible circumstances to live a productive,
triumphant life. Free me from fear and be my source of
strength and inspiration. Amen.

The One Who Doesn't Change

As for man, his days are like grass, he flourishes like a flower
of the field; the wind blows over it and it is gone, and its
place remembers it no more.
—Psalm 103:15-16

Jesus Christ is the same yesterday and today and forever.
—Hebrews 13:8

In 1847, in a little city south of Edinburgh, Scotland, Henry Lyte wrote the hymn "Abide with Me." Lyte had suffered some terrible personal losses. The first verse sets the tone for his well-known song:

Abide with me; fast falls the eventide;
the darkness deepens; Lord, with me abide.
When other helpers fail and comforts flee,
Help of the helpless, O abide with me.

I thought of that hymn as we viewed the Scottish landscape near Edinburgh some years ago from the vantage point of King Arthur's seat after a long climb from a scenic lane below. Other words from that hymn, "Change and decay in all around I see," had come back to me often during our travels. Here in Edinburgh, a city with origins in the thirteenth century, we'd visited St. Giles' Cathedral, where John Knox had preached; heard bagpipers playing in the misty rain in the courtyard of the old castle; and walked the dark brick and cobblestone streets where the authors Stevenson, Scott, and Burns are memorialized in a fascinating museum.

Changes take place from century to century, sometimes like the snap of a finger. We must know and understand history to recognize what is happening in the present. Because we so often ignore history, it repeats itself when it shouldn't. History is full of prophetic messages. In his book *Future Shock*, Alvin Toffler warns readers to be alert to change, lest they find themselves unable to comprehend or tolerate it.

In some European countries, we saw the changes necessitated by the bombings of World War II. Much had been rebuilt, but there were still ruined cities, bombed-out buildings, and graveyards where military personnel and prisoners of war lay slowly decaying.

We picked shrapnel out of bullet holes in the church in Noyen, France, across from the home in which John Calvin was reared. That morning, we were the only visitors to tour Calvin's house and play his old pump organ. Calvin—a mover and a shaker in Geneva and in the Protestant Reformation—had been forgotten or disowned by the people of his birthplace. And for Protestant tourists, Noyen was too far out of the way.

I was especially aware of change when we toured Pearl Harbor several years ago. I was in college when the terrible bombing occurred. I remember the announcement of the bombing and President Roosevelt's declaration of war. The world changed. Hatred reared its ugly head. No one knew what would happen next. In California, we had air raid drills; we went to work in the shipyards. We said goodbye to friends, some of whom did not return alive.

Yet some events that were earth-shaking years ago are forgotten today. In our concentration on growth and progress, we have nearly succeeded in burying the past, just as surely as some ancient cities now lie unknown below modern ones.

When I view the mad scramble to cover the good earth in my rural area with asphalt, I picture the lovely orchards and wildflowers of years past. If my homesite is someday covered with cement, I'd like people to know that camellias and roses once grew there, and that little children played happily in the walnut grove. I am thankful for historians, geologists, anthropologists, and genealogists who probe, discover, and analyze the past. They tell us how things once were.

Granted, not all change is caused by humans. Wind, rain, tides, and earthquakes alter the face of the earth. But for each change we do cause, we need to know what we are changing and why. Otherwise, we will never recognize the contrast between our ever-changing life and the changelessness of our Creator.

It is humbling to realize how short our time is on this earth. Each of us is but a blip on the screen of history. Under the stone floor of Westminster Abbey, many great statesmen, authors, poets, and composers lie buried. They once set policies for nations and inspired people with their works. Now all the kings of old, the czars and dictators, the oppressed and persecuted, the peons and peasants, our forebears—are gone, all gone. Empires have risen and fallen. Civilizations have thrived and been wiped out. Ideologies and philosophies have come and gone.

In my high school auditorium, a quote from Shakespeare's *As You Like It* was engraved in large letters above the stage:

All the world's a stage,
And all the men and women merely players.
They have their exits and their entrances,
And one man in his time plays many parts.

Generations of students came and went, reminded of their own mortality.

Does this litany of change and decay depress you? It could, but it could also inspire thankfulness, appreciation, tremendous joy, and relief. Through it all there is one who doesn't change. We can depend on it. Christians can experience the truth that God is ever-loving, ever-faithful, ever beside us, ever our heavenly Father and Comforter. Jesus Christ is the same yesterday, today, and forever. And one day he will usher in a new order, where all the change and decay of this life will be forever lost in the new kingdom.

Lyte knew this truth even in his pain and heartache. He said it this way:

I fear no foe with you at hand to bless;
though ills have weight, and tears their bitterness.
Where is death's sting, Where, grave, your victory?
I triumph still, if you abide with me.

Dear Jesus, I thank you that when the sight of change and decay depresses me I can turn to you—who are the same yesterday, today, and forever—and know that through all the changes in this life, we are assured of your promise of a new heaven and earth, where we will be with you permanently. Amen.

The Tipsy Pigeon

---

*Yet the LORD longs to be gracious to you; he rises to
show you compassion.*
—Isaiah 30:18

*And [God] passed in front of Moses, proclaiming, "The
LORD, the LORD, the compassionate and gracious God, slow
to anger, abounding in love and faithfulness...."*
—Exodus 34:6

We walked down the steps to a restaurant in Folkestone, England, just as a policeman was coming out. It was nearly eight o'clock in the evening, and my husband and I, with our companion couple, were tired after a long day of sightseeing. We asked the bobby about the eatery, and he replied without hesitation, "The best; you'll love it."

That's what the host and hostess at our lovely bed and breakfast had said. The next morning we would drive over to Dover and cross the Channel back to France. Right now we were hungry for a good meal.

So here we were at the Tipsy Pigeon, greeted like long-lost friends by the young couple who ran the place. Because they were ready to close, they could have turned us away, but they were pleasant and up-front with us. We would have to wait a while, but if we had time for that, they would serve us a delicious meal. And it was—steak, avocado salad with scampi, mushroom soup, and more. What struck us even more than the food, however, was the graciousness of the proprietors. We sat for a long time, enjoying the warmth of their hospitality. Was everything all right? Could they bring more? Were we happy? It wasn't a phony politeness with a tip in mind, but a sincere attempt to be accommodating and hospitable.

We noticed the same gracious attitude in our travels all over the Philippines as guests of the Bureau of Agricultural Extension. Government leaders as well as poor field workers showed it. People on the street would stop to ask us whether we liked their country and wish us a good day. One day we were treated to seven full-course meals, beginning early in the morning. Some were in the homes of mayors, others in the homes-on-stilts of frugal, hard-working rice farmers. Their sons had gone for a year of training in the States, and the parents and leaders expressed their gratitude by waiting on us and giving us gifts. They did not eat with us, but stood at our sides to serve us. It was embarrassing that they felt so honored by our group's presence. We knew that on many occasions the people could not afford the food they served us.

In contrast, we found people in some countries rude and unfriendly. In our own country, we've all experienced clerks who act as though they are doing us a favor by waiting on us; doctors who are unapologetic about being an hour late for our appointment; nasty phone callers; kids and parents who sass each other; people who make hurtful, racially-biased remarks; those who give curt replies with unsmiling faces.

Are courtesy and graciousness bred in people? Are they learned behaviors? Are they racial, regional, or religious traits? In the warm experiences we had throughout our travels, politeness wasn't stilted—like that of a TV butler who, if given the chance, would dump the food on the heads of those he serves. It didn't seem to matter, either, whether our friendly hosts were religious people.

Isn't it ironic that irreligious people can be more gracious than those who claim to be imitators of Christ? Within the body of Christ, people sometimes get so caught up in issues not germane to the essential task of the church that they are unfriendly and ungracious to those who do not think as they do. They snub fellow church members. They walk by them as if they don't exist. They don't want them to have offices in the church. If God practiced that kind of selective graciousness, we would all be doomed to the unforgiving heat of Hades.

My husband noted that in the numerous meetings he had to attend at the public college where he taught, people were much more tolerant of those with differing points of view than at meetings he had to attend at church. Tolerant not in the sense of compromising the truth, but in graciously listening to other points of view and respecting persons who differed.

Of all people, the Christian, who has experienced the undeserved grace and mercy of a loving God, should be most gracious to others, especially those who are brothers and sisters in Christ. Graciousness springs from love. It seeps, imperceptibly, into our attitudes and behavior toward others. It warms our relationships. It erases angry scowls and softens hearts. It shows itself in mercy and forgiveness, compassion and kindness.

I don't know whether Shakespeare was a Christian, but he understood what we often forget:

The quality of mercy is not strain'd.
It droppeth as the gentle rain from heaven
Upon the place beneath. It is twice blest:
It blesseth him that gives and him that takes.

But mercy is above this sceptred sway;
It is enthroned in the hearts of kings;
It is an attribute to God himself.
(*The Merchant of Venice*)

We have a compassionate and gracious God. We should mirror God in all our actions. The marvelous grace God shows to us should filter down softly into the nooks and crannies of our hearts and touch every part of our lives. I think that's what God wants to happen.

Lord, help me to treat others with the wonderful compassion
and grace you have shown me all through my life.
May my behavior toward others be motivated by a
loving and caring heart. Amen.

It's Mine, All Mine!

Do you not know that your body is a temple of the Holy
Spirit, who is in you, whom you have received from God?
You are not your own; you were bought at a price.
—*1 Corinthians 6:19-20*

And he is the head of the body, the church . . . so that in
everything he might have the supremacy.
—*Colossians 1:18*

The sound is familiar. Two little ones are tugging at the same toy, one shouting, "It's mine," and the other protesting, "No, it's mine!" Back and forth they yank until one prevails or an adult intervenes.

Kids' stuff, isn't it? Selfish, jealous little kids who want the biggest and best of everything. They'll punch each other for a sticky piece of candy, grab a swing that someone else is about to sit on, squeeze in at the front of a line, and shout cruel things at those who interfere.

We know they'll grow up physically, but will they outgrow the "gimme syndrome"? Many do, and they become gracious, selfless adults. Others spend the rest of their lives acting like children. The only things that change are what they fight over and how they go about getting it. It's like the wife describing her and her husband's possessions this way: "What's mine is mine and I'll keep it; what's his is mine and I'll take it; what's ours is mine and he better believe it!"

Seeds of selfishness lie in all of us. They may lie dormant for a while, but then they bloom. We fight for our rights, grab the best seats at the stadium or church, grasp for power and influence, and put others down to build ourselves up. We see "gimme" fights going on at department store sales, in political campaigns, in the way people drive on a busy highway, in the push-and-shove antics of some concert-goers, in our need to triumph in an argument. It's a mind-set of possession and entitlement—"I had it first," "The road is mine," "I paid good money to get in here," or "This job belongs to me."

Abortion rights activists carry placards saying, "Don't tell me what I can do; it's my body." Stuntmen proclaim their right to perform dangerous acts because their bodies belong to them. Drunkards and drug addicts tout their right to drink and use whatever they please. Teenagers tell parents to stay out of their business. In the "me generation," people are free to exploit sex, produce pornography, live together without a marriage license, choose their own lifestyle and sexual preference.

We are reaping the rotten fruit of that freedom—of the misconception that we are captains of our souls, that we belong to ourselves. Scripture rebukes us all saying, "Do you not know that your body is a temple of the Holy Spirit? . . . You are not your own." Your body does not belong to you. The right to disobey God's laws is not yours.

God's Word tells us to get rid of our possessive tendencies. Turn the other cheek, it says. Don't sue or go to court; take the loss. The first shall be last, and the last shall be first. Peacemakers, the meek, the pure in heart, the merciful, and the poor in spirit will inherit the earth and the kingdom of God.

Possessiveness is a real danger, especially in the church, where it can be cloaked in piety. Sometimes churches decide who may join based on whether the inquirers think and act as the church's members do. Sometimes church officers have their own agenda for the church's direction, and they are not above using manipulation and deceit to get their way. True progress toward the biblical vision for Christ's church is viewed with suspicion and fear.

Some members claim certain church programs as their own. I began to feel I was doing that after having taught a junior high class for more than twenty years. Emotionally, it was my class. It is an age group I love and feel comfortable with. But I gave it up. My replacement did a wonderful job and was given the opportunity he needed in his new church.

The church is not mine. Its programs are not mine. We are all necessary components of the body of Christ. And if the church is to function properly, we should all be seeking to serve—not seeking power. If we act like we own the church, we need to remember that Christ built it. It will stand long after we have strutted our stuff and left the scene.

Nothing is really ours—not our possessions, our children, our bodies, our homes, our churches, or our greatest plans. Everything is Christ's. We'd live happier lives remembering that.

Lord Jesus, when I'm tempted to count my possessions,
remind me that I own nothing, that everything is yours, and
that what I have is on loan from you to be used as a trust.
I rejoice that you are the head of the church and are
sovereign over all. Amen.

Holy Huddles

Therefore, prepare your minds for action; be self-controlled;
set your hope fully on the grace to be given you when
Jesus Christ is revealed.
—1 Peter 1:13

Whenever I watch a football game, I am curious about what goes on in the team huddles, and I admire the players' sustained enthusiasm as they huddle together.

Huddles convey a sense of urgency, as the team sets its plan of attack. The players aren't discussing a striking blonde in the second row on the fifty-yard line or the latest stock market reports. They're talking football—this game at this moment. They're playing hard because their future is at stake.

The clock runs down on the short time-out. The players crouch low, arms around each other. Suddenly they shout, slap each other on the back, and rush to their positions. The game goes on, losing little momentum from the brief interlude.

But what if each time a team got into a huddle, they called for coffee or beer, and "chewed the fat" for fifteen minutes? They might talk about the game, but they'd also look around at the people in the stands, show off for the spectators, bicker about who's getting the most attention, and argue about things not essential to the game. And what if they got back into position only to launch into new arguments—and then called for another time-out?

Certainly the fans would holler and boo the players! The stands would empty out, and spectators would demand a refund. The game would lose its charm, and football, as we know it, would disappear.

The Christian life is something like a game. The Bible speaks of it as a race. It's serious business. The church is a gathering of believers intent on winning the prize. Winning demands that people commit themselves to victory, knowing, as Christ said, that the church will stand and the gates of hell will not prevail against it.

Christ's church has huddles, too—holy huddles. Members come together to expedite the work of the kingdom. The church must have a game plan, a course of action to bring the world—the spectators in the bleachers—to Christ. Members are full of enthusiasm to get to their assigned positions—the ones in which their gifts lie—and go to it. Planning—purposeful, resolute, action-oriented, and conducted in an atmosphere of communion and fellowship—is necessary. The momentum of church life does not suffer because of the huddles.

But suppose, again, that the players in the church huddle are distracted, disgruntled members who are more interested in their self-image than in the image of Christ. It happens, you know. Meetings drag on aimlessly; volunteers are few; pertinent discussion is diverted by gossip, doubt, and lack of insight into the power of the Holy Spirit. Matters not relevant to the church's mission become the focus of debate. The huddles go on and on, and the spectators—those looking to the church to fill the void in their lives or inactive members always ready to condemn the church—desert the pews because the players have missed the point of the game. The church is going nowhere. It's full of fighting and mean-spiritedness; it offers only cheap grace.

When the church and its members conduct unholy huddles, no longer passionate about gathering God's children, huddles become social clubs for "holy" people steeped in a tradition of exclusiveness, dogma, and ecclesiastical babble.

But are there no holy huddles? Yes. Envision this: when committee members meet, they leave their biases and hang-ups at home. Like football players, they encircle one another with hearts of love. They pray together to seek the will of God. They concentrate on making plans and decisions that are best for the congregation and for the cause of Christ. They listen to each other in a spirit of tolerance and Christian fellowship. They speak to build up, not to tear down. They speak the truth in love, honesty, and good faith. They examine their motives and submit their thoughts and decisions to the scrutiny of a God who knows them very well.

God blesses this kind of huddle. And when the huddle is over, members get back into position to play the most important game of their lives.

Dear Father, I'd like to be the kind of church member who reaches out to others in Christian fellowship. May my motives always be holy, and may I seek to do what is best for your church and your kingdom. Amen.

The Other Side of the Mountain

Every prudent man acts out of knowledge,
but a fool exposes his folly.
—*Proverbs 13:16*

In the Bible, references to wonder, understanding, and knowledge always seem to be made in the context of wisdom about and from God. That's as it should be. The Bible is inspired by God to teach the way of salvation, God's laws and will, and the way to walk.

All knowledge is from God. To truly understand anything in this world, we need to remember that. The Bible tells us to get knowledge, and with it, understanding. We must be diligent students of the Bible, eager to learn.

Unfortunately, some Christians use the argument that all knowledge is from God to disparage the value of learning from other sources. Everything we need to know, they say, is in the Bible. They don't value higher education, though they readily use the discoveries of advanced scientific study, including those made by non-Christians. They use the services of medical specialists, lawyers, accountants, and other professionals who have spent years in advanced study. Yet at the same time, they shun the arts—poetry, symphonies, paintings, drama—unless it is what they call "Christian." They forget that God gave men and women artistic talents to glorify him and enrich their lives. Often these people fear education because it may cause them to change their thinking.

Such people forget that God *first* revealed himself in nature. Only because people sinned did God's second revelation, the Bible, become necessary. For Christians, the Bible is the rule of life, the revelation by which we live. But that beautiful world out there is right at our fingertips, filled with the creative touch of God, abundant with things to learn and explore. Culture is not a dirty word. It is, rather, the sum of the accomplishments, discoveries, creations, traditions, and spiritual tenor of the people.

I'm disheartened when I see Christians disdaining investigation, scholarship, and just plain curiosity. The latter may have killed the cat, but a lack of it impoverishes the mind and soul. Of all people, Christians should be most eager to learn about everything around them. Like the bear who "went over the mountain to see what he could see," we should be excited to explore the universe, to see the other side of the mountain, to learn about the things God put into this world for us to enjoy. I feel sorry for those who rob themselves of the pleasures of learning new ideas and seeing new places, of seeking answers to questions and finding new adventures.

Parents should model a holy curiosity to their children early in life. They should encourage their children to ask all kinds of questions, to think, and to explore. Families should sit around talking, asking questions, and looking up answers in the encyclopedia. At dinner years ago, one of our children spotted a praying mantis on the ceiling. Soon we were all huddled around a microscope as my husband explained the insect's anatomy to our wide-eyed youngsters. They listened quietly and asked questions for an hour.

On our family vacations, my husband often pointed out alluvial fans and other geological features to our children. Traveling gives families the opportunity to share stories, poems, interesting information, and new experiences. On one of our trips, my husband suddenly turned off a smooth highway onto a bumpy dirt road. As we quickly rolled up windows, I asked him why we had turned onto a road with no mileage or direction signs. I should have guessed his answer: "Because it's there, and because I wonder where it goes," he grinned. Twenty miles later, we had forded seventeen rivulets of water, each one wider than the last—and we had encountered some of the prettiest countryside we'd ever seen.

Children need to learn early—in and out of school—to ask why, how, when, and where. A child who talks about being bored either is not being challenged or has a habit of indifference and an absence of vision. Or perhaps he has parents who squelch his natural curiosity—who fear he will lose his faith if he thinks and exposes his mind to the unknown.

Samuel Johnson said, "The gratification of curiosity rather frees us of uneasiness, than confers pleasure. We are more pained by ignorance than delighted by instruction. Curiosity is the thirst of the soul."

God asked Job many questions about the mysteries of nature, pointing out Job's inability to probe them. He did this not to discourage investigation, but to put Job in his place. God might have asked Job, "Can you sit on the moon and walk in outer space?" Today the answer would be yes—not because humans were trying to be like God or will ever unravel the intricacies of nature, but because there was something to learn and because someone was curious enough to study and experiment and develop the technical knowledge. Most astronauts come back from their heavenly rides with faith in God reaffirmed.

If God brought you some beautifully wrapped presents, wouldn't you open them with curiosity and thanksgiving? The universe is God's gift to us to open and explore. There are discoveries to be made, symphonies to compose, and stories to write.

We take for granted our household conveniences, cars, computers, architecturally stunning buildings, electricity, phones, and atomic energy. We have these things only because people were curious enough to discover the resources God placed in the world—because they wondered what was on the other side of the mountain.

Lord, your world is fascinating and beautiful. Make me curious to explore your creation and learn more about you. Thank you for those who carefully use the earth's resources to make life more interesting and beneficial for all. Amen.

Joy

Surely you have granted him eternal blessings and made
him glad with the joy of your presence.
—Psalm 21:6

Restore to me the joy of your salvation.
—Psalm 51:12

The prospect of the righteous is joy.
—Proverbs 10:28

Perhaps you will disagree with some thoughts I have about joy. They are personal and unproven, though I find biblical foundation for them.

While reading D. Martyn Lloyd-Jones's *Studies in the Sermon on the Mount*, I was often reminded that Christ's words in Matthew were written specifically for Christians. Non-Christians often quote the beatitude about peacemakers to justify a dovish reaction to war. Though we certainly don't condone all wars, Christians know that the peace spoken of in the beatitudes is different from today's cessation-of-war interactions between nations.

Similarly, I believe joy is a form of spiritual contentment and happiness that only Christians can experience. The dictionary's synonyms for joy are good fortune, delight, gaiety, bliss, enjoyment, and happiness; but the Bible seems to speak of joy in the context of the spiritual.

I think of joy as the deep-down emotional condition of a heart and soul in tune with their Maker and Savior. From this heart-soul set come pleasure, gladness, fellowship, kinship, friendliness, and felicity.

Joy makes us genuinely happy. It takes the rough edges off sadness by joining hands with peace to make us tranquil, secure, and of one accord. Psalm 30:5 says, "Weeping may remain for a night, but rejoicing comes in the morning." I don't think this verse is talking about a magic twenty-four-hour period in which grief suddenly turns to gladness. Nor is it speaking about a dance-around-the-room kind of happiness. Yet the grief over a loved one's death can intensify the joy of being a Christian.

I don't think of joy as the comic side of happiness or as the hearty laughter in casual conversation. I think of it as soft and quiet and deep. It says that all is well. God is in control. Sometimes it's like the candy bar advertised as "indescribably delicious." My salvation in Christ is an indescribably wonderful gift from God; it is pure joy.

Why do I find great joy in my children and grandchildren? I think it is because they are Christians, precious gifts from God—a big bonus from God's storehouse of love. Were I not a Christian, I might think it was because I had created some pretty nice people and deserve what I produced. True joy in family is not something to boast about, but to be thankful for.

Joy has been described as "the royal standard floating from the flagstaff of the heart telling us that the King is in residence." Isn't that a beautiful picture? Joy is an announcement of the song the soul is singing.

Hebrews 12:2 says that Jesus could endure the cross and scorn its shame because of the joy set before him in redeeming his own and contemplating his future glory. In Galatians 5:22, Paul lists joy among the fruit of the Spirit. It keeps company with love, peace, patience, gentleness, and other quiet virtues.

A national news magazine recently ran a full-page advertisement for B and B Liqueur. The drink is labeled the "joie de vivre . . . a joyous celebration of life's unexpected moments—moments meant for B and B." How sad to define joy as a slug from a bottle of booze. How sad, too, that people often confuse joy with partying, winning the lottery, or watching a ball game.

Reactions to deep-seated joy vary. After Moses and Aaron blessed the Israelites, the people "shouted for joy and fell facedown" (Lev. 9:24). When Solomon was acknowledged as king in 1 Chronicles 29:22, the people ate and drank with great joy. In the Psalms we learn that the Israelites sang and danced for joy. In other passages people demonstrate joy by feasting, giving presents, shouting, praying, and being anointed with the oil of joy.

The Bible characterizes joy as complete, lasting, inexpressible, and glorious. Joy cannot be taken away from us (John 16:22), but it can be shared with others. It is given by the Holy Spirit (1 Thess. 1:6).

Hymns of the church often express the joy Christians have been given. Think about these words:

> Joys are flowing like a river since the Comforter has come.
> He abides with us forever, makes the trusting heart his home.

Or the stirring words of "How Great Thou Art":

> When Christ shall come, with shout of acclamation,
> and claim his own, what joy shall fill my heart!

One of my favorite writers—C. S. Lewis—wrote a book about grieving called *Surprised by Joy*. In it he says, "Joy is distinct not only from pleasure in general but even from aesthetic pleasure. It must have the stab, the pang, the inconsolable longing. . . . I sometimes wonder whether all pleasures are not substitutes for joy." In his *Letters to Malcolm*, Lewis says, "In this world, everything is upside down. That which, if it could be prolonged here, would be truancy, is likest that which in a better country is the End of ends. Joy is the serious business of heaven."

I am not interested in proving my theory that true joy can be experienced only by Christians. I'd just like to offer true joy, in the name of Christ, to all who are searching for permanent pleasure. You have no idea how beautiful and satisfying joy is until it settles down warmly in your heart and soul and brings you peace.

Dear Jesus, thank you for the joy you gave me through salvation in your precious name. May all who seek joy know that it can be found only in you, and may they give their hearts to you in repentance and faith. Amen.

Go For It!

Never be lacking in zeal, but keep your spiritual fervor.
—Romans 12:11

It is fine to be zealous, providing the purpose is good, and to
be so always and not just when I am with you.
—Galatians 4:18

Read 2 Corinthians 8:16–9:3, Paul's challenge to
the church to give enthusiastically.

One beautiful spring afternoon we took some friends to a fiddlers' jamboree in northern California. The whole farming community for miles around turned out for the long-awaited event. You could easily tell who the locals were. Some men, faces wrinkled and dry from the burning sun, wore wide-legged pants, full-yoked cowboy shirts, pointed boots, and well-worn western hats. Others had long, ponytailed hair, walrus-look mustaches, and scruffy red beards. Women wore everything from simple cotton dresses and bobby socks to cowgirl clothes.

People greeted each other with slaps and hugs as they gathered around the refreshment stand. When the emcee finally jumped to the stage, he shouted to the participants, "You all get your numbers [registration tags] and expedite your bods to the platform." Everyone followed orders and took their places.

Then it began. A night of foot-stomping, finger-snapping, "Wahoo"-shouting fun. Fiddlers made their instruments whine and plead, cry and laugh, their bows sucking sound from the fragile strings. Guitars vibrated; banjos plucked. A bass player slapped, yanked, and two-fingered his strings with silly abandon. A young lad happily banged on an old washboard as he swayed back and forth. Performers laughed and talked as they shared their music with the receptive audience. They were so enthusiastic that they played on into the night until dawn broke in the eastern sky.

We noticed the same kind of enthusiasm at the international Dixieland Jazz Festival in Sacramento. Even though the day was hot and the air-conditioning was minimal, the musicians loved what they were doing.

Their good mood was as contagious as their music. Everyone joined the celebration of rhythmic foot tapping.

If you like sports, you experience the same thing at a ball game. The crowd screams wildly; cheerleaders jump high into the air. The electric atmosphere is charged by the fans' instant reactions to every play.

When I witness this kind of enthusiasm, I wish we could have more of it in the church—not just in hearty singing, but in the worshipers' general mood and reaction. If, as Galatians says, "it is fine to be zealous, providing the purpose is good," imagine what some holy enthusiasm could do for our worship and work in the church.

If we can sit at a ball game for three or four hours, even when not much is happening, and leave the park full of spirited talk about the game, why can't we sit in church for an hour without falling asleep or looking bored? If a ball game goes into overtime, people are excited and think they're getting their money's worth, but when the preacher goes five minutes over, people become edgy and critical. I read recently of a "pray-and-dash twenty-two minute service" planned by a minister in Florida. It's supposedly a spiritual fast food restaurant, a challenge to an "outdated tradition." The service is planned down to the second—two hymns, an eight-minute sermon, some prayers and Scripture reading, and out the door you go. At exactly 8:22 a.m. the Sabbath is over and the worshipers are free to do less boring things.

The hymn "Spirit of God, Dwell Thou Within My Heart" speaks of a "holy passion filling all my frame." That is what we need. A passion for God's presence, for the Word, for praise and service. I've seen people make fools of themselves on the televised lottery spins. If they hit the jackpot, they jump, cry, hug, and swoon. Think a moment. We have the greatest gift anyone could ever have—a spiritual jackpot. Nothing can begin to equal it. Do we react with a whoop and a holler?

It seems that the more sophisticated we become, the more experienced we are at living in a complex society, and the more cynical we are about government red tape and dirty politics, the more we carry our criticism and suspicions over into the church. We don't want to be told hard things in church. We don't want to live under the policies of the denomination to which we belong. We want to punch a remote control button to turn off everything we don't like.

Instead of embracing attempts by our church leaders to define our vision and mission, we pooh-pooh training sessions, congregational meetings, and seminars. We piously announce that setting goals mini-mizes and interferes with the work of the Holy Spirit. A critical spirit, suspicion of every new idea, cynicism, indifference—these are things that dampen the work of the Holy Spirit and hurt the church of Jesus Christ.

If we make the church an exclusive club for those who think as we do and ignore the Great Commission to reach out to our community, we lack the passion for God and others that is the meat of the gospel.

The same is true in our personal lives. We cannot say we are zealous about our faith—about that immensely sacrificial gift Christ gave us—if we don't show it with a grateful life, a positive frame of mind, a praising spirit, and a loving heart.

Ralph Waldo Emerson said, "Nothing great was ever achieved without enthusiasm. The sense of this word among the Greeks affords the noblest definition of it: enthusiasm signifies 'God is Us.'"

If we can shout until we're hoarse about a ball game or concert, why not about a gift that has forever changed our lives and ensures a life forever with God in heaven? That's something to get excited about!

Lord, help me put first things first. Fill me with enthusiasm and a holy resolve to work in your church and to appreciate what others are striving to do in your kingdom. Amen.

Time to Meditate

Oh, how I love your law! I meditate on it all day long.
—Psalm 119:97

He leads me beside quiet waters, he restores my soul.
—Psalm 23:2

People today seem to be in a mad scramble to survive. The fast lane of life is crowded with people dashing hectically from one activity to another. They weave recklessly in and out like drivers on busy freeways. How many really know where they are going? In the slow lane we seem to find only philosophers, the elderly, the ill or handicapped, and sleeping babies.

Many families no longer take time to eat or talk together. There are too many meetings to attend, ball games to enjoy, and TV programs to watch. Weekends are dedicated to sports, parties, and shopping. Bridges and mountain peaks are now used as takeoff points for bungee jumpers and hang gliders. Beautiful hillsides are marred and eroded by dirt bikes roaring up and down their fragile slopes.

Christian families, too, are caught up in the insane pace of modern living. Their busy schedules are often justified because they are filled with church or Christian school activities. But family prayers and devotions suffer. The family altar is covered with computer paper, broken resolves, and neglected Bible readings.

In his poem "Leisure," William Henry Davies wrote,

What is this life if, full of care,
We have no time to stand and stare.

No time to stand beneath the boughs
And stare as long as sheep or cows.

A poor life this if, full of care,
We have no time to stand and stare.

And William Wordsworth lamented,

> The world is too much with us; late and soon,
> Getting and spending, we lay waste our powers:
> Little we see in Nature that is ours;
> We have given our hearts away, a sordid boon!

In an attempt to find time to meditate and contemplate, some of England's romantic poets and some Early American essayists and poets withdrew from a life full of care. Thoreau had Walden Pond and Emerson his cloistered room with desk and pen. William Butler Yeats had his Lake Isle of Innisfree, about which he wrote,

> I will arise and go now, and go to Innisfree,
> And a small cabin build there, of clay and wattles made;
> Nine bean rows will I have there, a hive for the honey bee,
> And live alone in the bee-loud glade.
>
> And I shall have some peace there, for peace comes dropping slow,
> Dropping from the veils of the morning to where the cricket sings;
> There midnight's all a glimmer, and noon a purple glow,
> And evening full of the linnet's wings.

We tend to call that kind of lifestyle, and the writing it produces, escapism. Poets and essayists are dubbed idealists, dreamers, cowards, unproductive members of society. That may be true of some. But often, they—rather than our political and economic leaders—see most clearly the ills of society. The temperature of the world is often best taken not by the climatologists, but by the thinkers, whose thermometers are strategically placed in the soul of society.

Why are people afraid of silence? Why do pauses in conversation cause panic? Why do requests for silent prayers cause awkwardness and discomfort? I think it is because we lack the ability to meditate, to withdraw quietly from our cares and concerns to ponder God and his magnificent universe. This is often true for me when I pray. All of a sudden I lose my train of thought, and I'm wondering whether I paid the bill to the Board of Equalization or whether it's going to be foggy tomorrow morning. Even though I live alone, I find it difficult to listen for the still, small voice of God.

Perhaps the long, enforced silence that monks and nuns experience in their cloistered sanctuaries is too much for us. I remember feeling almost claustrophobic when I read *The Nun's Story* by Kathryn Hulme. But I have heard of college students who retreated to a monastery for several days of quiet meditation and came back to school refreshed and changed. Maybe an experience like that, away from all our responsibilities and cares, is the best possible stress-reduction therapy.

Children need time away from school, sports practices, music and ballet lessons, and all the other extracurricular activities that can fetter them. They need to have time to lie on the grass, gaze at the sky, count the stars, and watch with awe as the moon illuminates the darkening night. They need to snuggle next to their parents' warm bodies and be read to. Adults need to cancel some party plans and walk silently through the woods. Christians need to draw apart, as Christ did, to read the Bible, meditate, and pray.

Francis Quarles said, "Meditation is the life of the soul; action is the soul of meditation; honor is the reward of action; so meditate that thou mayst do; so do that thou mayst have honor." Owen Felltham suggested, "Meditation is the soul's perspective glass, whereby, in her long removes, she discerneth God, as if He were nearer at hand."

Psalm 23 says our souls are restored when we let God lead us to the quiet waters. All our Bible study groups, coffee hours, and church programs are good in themselves, but we must learn to be comfortable all alone in the presence of God. Many people are terrified to step out of themselves, so to speak, and study their dependence on God. We need to meditate, to stand and stare. That's when we find God.

My soul is restless until I rest in you, dear Father. Draw me apart, alone with you, and let me hear you speak to me. Help me spend time in meditation and prayer. Amen.

Remembering

"Remember this, fix it in mind, take it to heart. . . .
Remember the former things."
—Isaiah 46:8

On my bed I remember you.
—Psalm 63:6

"What she has done [she poured perfume on Jesus] will
also be told, in memory of her."
—Matthew 26:13

Memory is the diary we carry within us. It is the treasurer of the mind. The brain fills its pages with all our reactions as we hear, see, feel, smell, and taste; as we make decisions; as we experience pain, happiness, sorrow, and a range of other emotions.

Memories can be sweet or bitter. They can be shared with large groups of people or enjoyed all alone. Sweet memories can be used to fill the lonely hours. And unpleasant memories can haunt the mind with past evils, with wasted time and lives, with hurts that will not go away. In Sonnet 30, Shakespeare mused,

> When to the sessions of sweet silent thought
> I summon up remembrance of things past,
> I sigh the lack of many a thing I sought,
> And with old woes new wail my dear time's waste.

Memory can play subtle tricks on us. The experience of *déjà vu* always leaves us baffled. An attempt to duplicate or relive a special memory often results in disappointment and sadness. Memories can come in a sudden flash—through a song, a touch, a fragrance—and disappear as quickly as a falling star.

Some psychologists say we remember what we choose to remember and push into the background what we'd rather forget. And yet, there are things we wish we could remember and other things we wish we could forget. Lady Macbeth's exclamation "Out, damned spot!" as she tries to erase the thought of her evil deed, exemplifies the frustration and pain we feel when the mind will not relinquish a torturous memory.

I believe it was Edith Schaeffer who said, "Memories are the archives in the museum of our minds." We all want those archives to be meaningful. My father died when I was four years old, and it has always saddened me that I have no memory of him. He baptized me, held me in his arms, played with me, and loved me. But I have no memory of his presence in my life.

That is why I've tried to fill my children's and grandchildren's lives with tangible memories. When our four children were growing up, I filled their baby books with information and remembrances, made each one a photo album, and updated their scrapbooks yearly. As they left home, their books went with them. During their post-college years, I wrote each child a book of about eighty pages called *I Remember* . . . . Each book was handwritten and contained pictures and special memories for that particular child. The book I wrote for Dan, who died in his late twenties, is in my bedside bookcase. I returned to it recently, after ten years, to write an update.

My husband and I received a delightfully unexpected reply to those memory books a few Christmases after we gave them. It was a handwritten, blue velvet-covered book from our children called *We Remember* . . . . In it, each of our three remaining children and their spouses recorded memories associated with our family. The stories were hilarious, sweet, grateful, and exaggerated, but not maudlin. They are small masterpieces, and I return to them often.

I also wrote a color-coded, indexed recipe book for each of the children, full of family and personal favorites. My husband illustrated each book with clever pen-and-ink drawings. When our son got married, he lamented, "I suppose since I'm a guy I don't get one of those cookbooks." We fooled him; he got one.

We need to preserve memories of cookies fresh from the oven, fun vacations, and good family times. But of more eternal consequence is spiritual memory—God's remembrance of us and our remembrance of God.

The Bible tells us to remember our Creator and to extol God's works, forgiveness, greatness, patience, and laws, which are meant for our safety and well-being. It tells us to remember to do good, especially to those in the household of faith. It tells us to remember to love our enemies, to meditate on God's Word, and to seek God. It tells us to remember the past and all God's promises to us.

The Bible also tells us that God remembers. The amazing thing about God's memory is that God can decide to forget. God may remember everything we do and every thought we have, but our Maker has promised that when we repent, he will remember our sins no more. When we forgive, we often don't forget. We hold grudges and nurture our injured feelings by remembering. God nurtures us by forgetting and holds nothing against us.

God remembers us and loves us. On judgment day, the unredeemed will stand condemned because God will remember all their sins. But the transgressions of those who believe will be forgotten. Isn't that a comforting thought? Doesn't it make the Christian life worth living joyfully? Doesn't it make our celebration of the Lord's Supper more meaningful? We come to the table sadly aware of our inability to please God perfectly, yet joyfully aware that through Christ's great sacrifice and gift of love we stand blameless before God.

I once asked my junior high class at church to write an epitaph for their tombstone, telling how they'd like to be remembered when they die. One kid wrote humorously, "Watch where you step." But another wrote, "She tried her very best to be God's child."

How do you want to be remembered? What would you put on your tombstone? More importantly, how will God remember you? What will God write on your forehead?

Thank you, Lord, for allowing me to remember with thanks the good events and experiences of my life and to learn lessons from the unpleasant ones. Thank you for remembering me in love and redemption and for forgetting the sins of the past. Amen.

Counting the Days

Teach us to number our days aright, that we may
gain a heart of wisdom.
—Psalm 90:12

"Is not wisdom found among the aged?"
—Job 12:12

The minister stepped to the pulpit, greeted the congregation, and announced the first song: "O Teach Thou Us to Count Our Days." I stared at him in disbelief. Didn't he know that most of these people were in their eighties and nineties? Count their days? These retirement home residents knew all about that. Some were heading into the final countdown.

As the worshipers in the chapel opened their hymnals, I looked around me. Some sat in wheelchairs. Others had pillows behind their backs. Some had shaky hands and stooped shoulders. Many used a cane. In just four rows, I counted twenty-six widows and five widowers.

The organist played an introduction to the psalm, and as the pastor directed the singing, people joined in:

> O teach Thou us to count our days
> And set our hearts on wisdom's ways;
> Turn, Lord, to us in our distress,
> In pity now Thy servants bless;
> Let mercy's dawn dispel our night,
> And all our day with joy be bright.

Some sang lustily, nodding agreement with each word. Some stared straight ahead, their mouths closed—could their minds no longer send the messages to form the words? Others sang falteringly or simply mouthed the words. Tears slipped down the cheeks of some.

The minister preached a sermon on sins and temptations peculiar to older people—disillusionment, self-pity, bitterness, doubt, and the desire to give up; anger with God, their children, or themselves; envy of others. He gently urged the congregation to count all their days and all their blessings, and to seek wisdom as they lived each day with God. As I listened to him and saw the audience's response, I realized that his choice of Psalm 90 was wise. I looked at the song's other verse:

So let there be on us bestowed
The beauty of the Lord our God;
The work accomplished by our hand
Establish Thou, and make it stand;
Yea, let our hopeful labor be
Established evermore by Thee.

We sang some more hymns, a few aged men took the offering, and the people began leaving the chapel. Some went directly to their rooms, but many lingered. They smiled and greeted one another. Couples held on to each other for support. Some singles did, too, as they hobbled or walked stiffly. Some were quite able mentally and physically. But all had been up-rooted from their old lives. They had given up their independence; their home; the church in which they had served faithfully; and the opportunity to travel, garden, work, and be near relatives.

In the large, lovely manor where they lived—some independently, and others with assistance—all felt a sense of protection and companionship. A few considered their ailments an indignity. Others were quite accepting, if not fatalistic, about their present circumstances and the fragility of life. Still others were able to joke about their aches and pains. None seemed to dwell on the their physical condition. Most had dressed attractively just to walk from their rooms or apartments to the chapel. One magnificently dressed woman called to a group standing nearby, "I'll see you at nine o'clock tomorrow morning for bridge," and ran down the hall, laughing and waving. She was eighty-five years old.

When I told a friend about my experience at the chapel, she observed, "With most of these people, their spiritual maturity so overshadows their physical and mental limitations that all one really sees is their inner beauty." They were counting their days in a truly biblical sense.

Most of us have done a lot of counting—counting the days until we're sixteen and can get a driver's license. Counting the days until we graduate or get married. Counting the days until the child within us is delivered or until the child we're adopting can join the family. Counting the days until we get a good job, until Christmas or vacation or the weekend. Counting the days until the children leave the nest, until we can retire, until the grandchild is born, until the Social Security check arrives. Maybe even counting the days until we're home with Jesus.

It is frightening to me how quickly days pass. Suddenly all the days we counted in anticipation of life's events become a lengthening shadow at the other end of life. How often have we "set our hearts on wisdom's ways?" Perhaps we should be more concerned with the quality than the quantity of our days.

We first learned to count as innocent children. As we grow older, we mature spiritually; with wisdom from God we learn to count with spiritual numbers. That's the kind of counting that really matters.

Teach me, Lord, to count my days and use them wisely.
Bless and comfort those who spend their days and nights in
pain or misery. As they contemplate leaving this life, may
they know that in heaven time will be no more, and you
will be their all in all. Amen.

Anchors, Storms, Battle Cries, and Shepherds

"The LORD is my strength and my song."
—Exodus 15:2

Speak to one another with psalms, hymns and spiritual songs.
—Ephesians 5:19

Nutritionists tell us we are what we eat. That's true for our bodies; but I have long felt that we are, in many of the important parts of our lives, what we sang and read as children. We are molded by our early perceptions of biblical truths. The hymns of my childhood have powerfully influenced my behavior, my ethical sense, and my philosophy of life.

As a vacation Bible school student at a neighborhood church, I remember singing, "Down in the dumps I'll never go" and thinking, "Dream on, kids—do you really think that's how life works?" I wonder whether that church wanted kids to think that life is one circus ride after another.

At my church, children sang about sturdy, meaty stuff. We were soldiers fighting the battle to end all battles. Stirring, 4/4-time songs challenged us to don the armor of the Lord. We sang, "Sound the battle cry! See the foe is nigh. . . . Rouse then, soldiers, rally round the banner." Singing these songs didn't make us think about guns and killing, as it does some children today. The impression left on me was that Christians are prevailers. One song ended with the dramatic question "Who is on the Lord's side? Who for him will go?" And we couldn't wait to answer, "By Thy grace divine, we are on the Lord's side. Savior, we are Thine." The awkward *thee*s, *thou*s, and *thine*s didn't bother us.

We were also sailors. We raised our voices high singing "In the good ship of the captain we are sailing o'er life's sea . . . heirs to earth's felicity." We didn't know what felicity was, but it sounded okay to us. Our songs were filled with nautical imagery: "my anchor holds," "from sinking sands he lifted me," "Jesus, Savior, pilot me," and "the Lord's our rock, in him we hide, a shelter in the time of storm." The lighthouse was bright and visible; Jesus was the shelter, our faith, the anchor.

Other songs emphasized our status as pilgrims ("I am a stranger here . . . on business for my king"); our rebellious nature ("I've wandered far away from God; now I'm coming home"); and the urgency of the gospel call ("Far and near the fields are teeming . . . Lord of harvest, send forth reapers").

Sometimes we got tongue-tied with all the *whithers* and *revealeths* and with phrases like "waft, waft," "treacherous shoal," "vanquished armies," "toiling flesh," and "schisms rent asunder." But we prevailed.

I grew up during the depression. My family was poor, but so were a lot of other people. Our family had no breadwinner. We learned about trust, hard work, and the seriousness of commitment. In those days, more young men entered the ministry, there were fewer forced marriages, and divorce was almost unheard of.

I can recall only a few times when we children dared make light of spiritual matters. Sometimes we laughed ourselves silly over the sound of the Ten Commandments read in Dutch (as was done in our church twice a month). We also went back and looked up Proverbs 7 when our mother skipped it in our nightly reading. We snickered over it but didn't understand it all.

Church was generally serious business. As children, we memorized reams of songs, Bible texts, and catechism answers. When our elders served communion, they wore dark suits and walked at a funeral pace. They were unsmiling. Children were separated from their parents during the Lord's Supper. That memory still depresses me; I'm so glad our communion services today celebrate a risen Christ rather than burying him over and over.

Yet our serious attitude toward church didn't make us somber children. All in all, we were good little soldiers of the cross. Happy ones, too. I felt surges of genuine joy in being a good person, because I knew that was the best way to be.

I never felt threatened by hell, though words such as "Almost persuaded; almost, but lost," gave me the chills. And songs of death were sometimes spooky: "When this poor, lisping, stammering tongue lies silent in the grave. . . ." I could just picture it—no body, only a tongue.

But there were so many triumphant songs that the combination was harmonious. We often sang "What a Friend We Have in Jesus," "'Tis So Sweet to Trust in Jesus," "Safe in the Arms of Jesus," and "Savior, Like a Shepherd Lead Us"—lovely hymns with comforting words.

The time in which I grew up; my family situation; my strong, trusting mother; and our family's emphasis on Bible reading and prayer—these factors taught me the importance of faith and commitment. The rewards of trust and obedience were attainable and deeply satisfying.

The songs I sang as a child and the spiritual guidance provided through materials like *Hurlbut's Story of the Bible Told for Young and Old* prepared me well for the trials and joys of my life. They have helped me lead my own children to Christ, bring the Word to others, and comfort fellow Christians. Let us hope contemporary music will do the same for today's children.

Times have changed. Perhaps affluence frees us to be less serious and more joyful. I like the celebratory mood in churches today. I like the new tunes foreign to my childhood. Many are deeply moving, encompassing many cultures and ethnic backgrounds. But churches today often imitate the style of the world, with loudspeakers, hand-held microphones, and the crooning of sentimental tunes. While some of today's repetitive "fluff" may leave us on an emotional, rhythmic high, it provides little to hold on to alone in the depths of the night.

We used to sing "From Greenland's icy mountains to India's coral strand . . . God calls us to deliver his land from error's chain." While a couple hundred people lay sleeping during our first family flight to Europe, I stayed awake all night, looking out the window at that long-awaited childhood scene and reliving the song's message. Staying awake that night was worth it.

Lord, thank you for the spiritual training I had at home and in church. Thank you for the psalms and hymns you inspired composers to write. Help parents to be diligent in teaching their children spiritually enriching songs and stories. Amen.

The Great Divide

*But our citizenship is in heaven. And we eagerly await a
Savior from there.*
—Philippians 3:20

Heaven has always been popular. Most people seem sure they are going there one day. People tell grieving youngsters that their deceased pets
have joined that immortal throng in doggie heaven. Irreligious people
claim confidently that their deceased loved ones have gone to heaven, as
though everyone is entitled. In reality, many people would find themselves out of sync and out of place in heaven.

Hell, on the other hand, is a place people do not discuss. Punishment
is unpopular. Fire-and-brimstone sermons may have scared people into
church a century ago, but hell is rarely discussed in mainline churches today. It is considered a dusty relic, the product of an ignorant, legalistic,
and superstitious mentality.

Though the concept of hell is passé today, the word itself is used fre-
quently—more often than *heaven*. In a newspaper story, a minister eulo-
gized a fellow clergyman as "one hell of a guy who was a fighter for the
things he believed in." Given all the references to hell in exclamations,
jokes, curses, and condemnations, you might think people actually believe
in it.

Few seem to sense the great antithesis between heaven and hell, the
yawning chasm that divides the two places—perhaps in distance, but
surely in purpose, entrance requirements, atmosphere, and living stan-
dards. Many have no knowledge of what heaven and hell are all about,
and they trample carelessly on holy ground. They talk about heaven and
hell as though with the punch of a button they can choose which one they
will inhabit.

The simple good news is that if we believe in Jesus Christ as Savior and
Lord and commit our lives to him in faith and service, he will take us to
heaven. The awful alternative is hell. There is no middle ground, no second chance, no manipulation of God's records, no pitting of mercy
against justice, no cajoling or placating the judge.

Society used to be more concerned with hell's punishment and heaven's
rewards. Past poets, philosophers, and theologians were consumed with

the significance of the antithesis. Medieval art often depicted the fall in the Garden of Eden and the fear of hell and darkness. Milton often thought about heaven and hell. In "Paradise Lost" he wrote,

> Which way shall I fly
> Infinite wrath and infinite despair?
> Which way I fly is hell; myself am hell;
> and in the lowest deep a lower deep
> still threatening to devour me, open wide—
> To which the hell I suffer seems a heaven.

Within the dusky aisles of Stanford University's lovely Memorial Chapel, inscriptions chosen by Mrs. Leland Stanford occupy special places along the walls. One inscription amid the chapel's mosaics and stained-glass windows reads,

> There is no narrowing so deadly as the narrowing of a man's horizon of spiritual things. No worse evil can befall him than in his course on earth to lose sight of Heaven. And it is not civilization that can prevent this; it is not civilization that can compensate for it. No widening of science, no possession of abstract truth can indemnify for an enfeebled hold on the highest central truths of humanity. What shall a man give in exchange for his soul?

C. S. Lewis described hell as "the separation from humanity—not parallel to heaven, it is darkness of the outer rim where beings fade away into non-entity."

The great divide—heaven and hell. Light and darkness. Good and evil.

Heaven and hell are not metaphysical concepts. They are real places. The Bible has not told us their locations except directionally—up and down—and this could be symbolic. I have heard ministers describe hell as a place of pain, suffering, and intense heat. I've also heard them wax eloquent about the structural beauty of heaven—the gold-paved streets, the precious gems, the jeweled mansions, the tiaras, and the crowns.

Somehow the physical descriptions don't interest me. I'm sure heaven will be beautiful and hell will epitomize evil and ugliness. My great sorrow is that Christ had to go to hell in order to bring me to heaven. My comfort is that he went willingly because he loves me. My joy is that mortals will finally live in perfection and harmony in heaven.

In that perfection we will not only be free of earth's encumbrances, but we will be free of all sin, living in the presence of God. Free to enjoy him forever as new creatures. Heaven will perfectly reflect God's beauty, truth, light, love, and joy. And hell will be completely removed from God's presence; none of God's attributes and characteristics will ever be present. That separation is the horror of hell.

The Bible says there are rewards and levels of honor in heaven. Yet to me the idea of being rewarded for living a life of thanks for receiving new life seems almost ironic. And since jealousy and competitiveness won't exist in heaven, will anyone except God know whether I'm a step higher or lower than anyone else in glory? I don't mean by this that we should try to get into heaven "by the skin of our teeth." But I have a hard time getting excited about the number of gems my crown will have or about my position in the heavenly order.

I do hope there will be a "grounds committee" in heaven and that God will put me on it. Then I will get down on my renewed knees and nurture the most beautiful roses you've ever seen. God will look at them, too . . . and at me . . . and smile.

Dear Father, I thank you that I can look forward to the joys of heaven and can be free of the fear of hell. Thank you for providing a place where all your children can spend eternity with you, living together, loving together, and enjoying you forever. Amen.

The Greatest Indignity: A Lenten Meditation

He was despised and rejected by men, a man of sorrows, and familiar with suffering. . . . He was pierced for our transgressions, he was crushed for our iniquities.
—Isaiah 53:3, 5

Then Pilate took Jesus and had him flogged. The soldiers twisted together a crown of thorns and put it on his head. . . . And they struck him in the face.
—John 19:1-3

If you have never had an upper or lower G.I. (gastrointestinal) test, be thankful, and know that you have avoided one of life's many indignities.

I had my first upper G.I. some years ago. Led to a cold little cubicle and handed one of those humiliating hospital gowns, I was told to undress and wait until I was called. I had forgotten my reading glasses, but that was okay since every magazine in the place was at least two years old. When I was finally called into the radiologist's "holy of holies," I hurried down the long hall, clinging desperately to the gown's rear opening. Other patients slunk past me, equally ill at ease in their blue-checked gowns.

I drank chalky barium and was told not to belch; that would spoil the test. Then I lay on a cold table while a heavyset man with a German accent and the appearance of an S.S. guard shouted orders at me. "You vill not breathe," he said. Was that a threat, an order, or a promise? "Hold it"—extra long pause—"Now breathe." Several trips back and forth to the chilly cubicle followed.

More barium. More orders. Back on the table for the last time, my skimpy gown in complete disarray, I got the order: "You vill breathe now." That's when I knew I'd live to get out of that place. The air was sweet as I exited, fully clothed but with a bruised self-esteem.

I can look back on that experience now with amusement. It was, I suppose, a necessity. It revealed the need for surgery.

But what of the many indignities suffered by those who are neglected, abused, persecuted, ignored, taunted, and dehumanized? What of the aged person left to die because he is no longer productive? What of the woman whose husband degrades her in public and emotionally and physically batters her in private? What of the child who is slapped and shaken and told she is no good? Or the woman who is raped and pushed from her car after being threatened with death? Or the poor little boy in cast-off clothes who is ridiculed by his classmates? Or the woman who has to stand in the welfare line because she was deserted by a husband who refuses to support her and the children?

What of the homeless? What of the teenage prostitute enslaved by a pimp? What of the early Christians sewn up in animal skins and thrown to the lions while their persecutors sat in the arena applauding? Or prisoners of war, stripped bare and paraded in front of leering guards? Or those who endure repeated racial harassment? Or victims of physical and mental handicaps who are taunted because they cannot control their bodies?

Horrible indignities like these occur all the time all over the world, a sordid part of the history of civilization. These experiences humiliate both body and soul. No one should have to endure them.

Yet, once upon a time, there was a king who ruled the entire world with his father, who was the creator of the universe. No ruler could have been more kind and generous to his subjects; he should have received their loving devotion. But the people rebelled, wanting the power to rule themselves. The father was therefore duty-bound to condemn his subjects to everlasting death. His justice demanded it.

But the father was a merciful ruler. He decided to send his son to take the renegade earthlings' punishment. The son, part of the divine triumvirate, went down to earth and lived a very unkingly life. He came as a baby who had to be diapered, and he lived with poor, sinful people. He bore all kinds of indignities and injustices. He brought the people the good news that he would take their place and cover their sins if they would believe in him. He told them his father loved them so much that he gave his only son to redeem them from the sentence of death.

The greatest indignity, however, was that, for all his work on earth, he was rejected, hated, and even betrayed by one of his own followers. He was condemned to die on a cross, while his enemies spat on him, taunted him, and reveled together. Worst of all, he suffered the forsaking of his father and the pangs of hell.

A myth about ancient gods and goddesses? No, my friend, this is the greatest piece of nonfiction ever published, the all-time best-selling story.

The greatest love led to the greatest indignity for the greatest good of the human race.

It makes an upper G.I. story sound like a picnic.

Dear Jesus, you were despised and rejected by men and forsaken by the Father. It grieves me that you had to suffer and die in my place. Thank you, Lord, for your sacrifice and for the salvation you gave me. Amen.

That's the Life!

*The mind of sinful man is death, but the mind controlled by
the Spirit is life and peace.*
—Romans 8:6

He who has the Son has life.
—1 John 5:12

Jesus answered, "I am the way and the truth and the life."
—John 14:6

"To be nineteen, to earn $5,000 a week, to drive around in a Jaguar, to
have your own horse, to decorate your home in Beverly Hills, to date
some of the most attractive men in town, to do what you've always
wanted to do—what more could any girl ask for?" This is the response a
fledgling actress gave several years ago to the question "What do you
consider to be the life?"

A popular professional athlete recently said he was tremendously
excited about the good life he was leading. He was making thirteen million dollars a year, he had a house with thirteen bathrooms, and he really
loved his fourth wife.

An elderly retired actress said she was having the time of her life—
three packs of cigarettes a day, good drinks, and nights full of parties. She
said she never thinks about death because she's living the life.

However, the material things of life do not attract some people. In fact,
for some, nothing in life is appealing. Macbeth walked the floor in the
black of night, muttering,

Out, out, brief candle!
Life's but a walking shadow, a poor player
That struts and frets his hour upon the stage
And then is heard no more. It is a tale
Told by an idiot, full of sound and fury,
Signifying nothing.

George Bernard Shaw claimed that "life is a disease; and the only difference between one man and another is the stage of the disease at which
he lives." Voltaire, in a similar mood, said, "I advise you to go on living

solely to enrage those who are paying your annuities. It is the only pleasure I have left." He was living but hadn't found life.

Men and women through the centuries have pondered the meaning of life, searching in vain for the good life. Some, finding life to be an empty shell, have, like Richard Cory, put a bullet through their head. Others have opted for slower suicide through drugs and liquor. Judas thought thirty pieces of silver was the life; then he went out to hang himself. Lot's wife was sure Sodom was the life; she became a chunk of salt. Adam and Eve thought forbidden fruit was the life; instead, they faced a death sentence.

How often do we grasp for "the chance of a lifetime," only to find ourselves reduced to sackcloth and ashes? Is life, then, a walking shadow, an idiot's tale, a terrible disease, a nothing?

How good it is to see Christ walk across the pages of time and hear him say, "A man's life does not consist in the abundance of his possessions" (Luke 12:15), and "I have come that [you] may have life, and have it to the full" (John 10:10). He tells us that life in him is abundant living, that he is life itself. He tells us that the good life has nothing to do with cigarettes, horses, a large bank account, a prosperous farm, or a lovely home. True life, he says, is living spiritually; the life is having the Son.

What does "having the Son" mean? It means that we are his; we are grafted into him. He is our life. He is our hope. Christ, who died to give us life, gives us a new language to speak. He comes to live in us permanently. He showers us with his promises, his love, his grace, and his Spirit. He gives meaning to our lives. He is our all in all. We, in turn, try to imitate him in a life of gratitude and praise.

In a recent Grammy Awards ceremony, a gospel singer invited the foot-tapping audience to join him in a song. The result was ludicrous and pathetic. The Hollywood "greats," who supposedly have everything a carnal mind can desire, were completely baffled as they mumbled words they did not comprehend: "I've got the peace that passes understanding down in my heart." The words were foreign. The audience needed an interpreter.

What happiness it is to sing these simple words of testimony: "Jesus is all the world to me—my life, my joy, my all."

What is the life? Being spiritually minded. Having the Son. That's the life!

Lord, there is no better life than one dedicated to you. I thank you that you have given me your Son, for in him I have life forever more. Amen.

The Bare Necessities

"Watch out! Be on your guard against all kinds of greed;
a man's life does not consist in the abundance
of his possessions."
—Luke 12:15

Jesus replied, "Foxes have holes and birds of the air have nests,
but the Son of Man has no place to lay his head."
—Luke 9:58

Those who grew up during the Great Depression can tell many stories about deprivation and poverty. Survivors of wars all over the world can describe the pain of growling, empty stomachs. Thousands of the world's people have died without the bare necessities.

The word *necessity* is a relative term whose meaning depends on its context. In a recent survey of hundreds of households with annual incomes over $100,000, people were asked what things beyond food, clothing, and shelter were necessities of life. Fifty-seven percent said they couldn't get by without a microwave; forty-nine percent listed a telephone answering service as a necessity; forty-two percent said a home computer is a must; and thirty-six percent couldn't make it without a VCR.

True, we live in a high-tech society. We need technical knowledge to get good jobs today. But long ago, in about 30 A.D., before machines were invented, a wealthy man asked Jesus how he might obtain eternal life. Jesus told him to sell everything and follow him. We know the sad ending. The young man walked away disappointed because he had great possessions. He thought he needed them. They meant more to him than the future life he had inquired after.

I grew up in the 1920s and 1930s with a mother who was widowed at forty-seven. She had eight children under the age of twenty-one. My father had been a minister, but ministerial pensions were in their infancy; my mother got less than five hundred dollars a year from the denomination. There was no Social Security, no health or life insurance, no assistance for needy dependents, no food stamp program. When we got holes in the soles of our shoes, we cut pieces of cardboard to fit inside. Sometimes we replaced the cardboard every evening. When I broke my glasses in the fourth grade, I patched them with wads of adhesive tape. None of us had our own bedroom or shoes to match each outfit. In fact, we had only a few outfits.

And yet, we got by. There was always food on the table. We used the public library. We played in the parks and on the beaches of our city. We took day trips to places with free admission. The older children helped out as they became wage earners. Some worked two or three jobs and still got good grades in school. I remember working in the school cafeteria in exchange for lunch and grading trigonometry papers (a subject I detested) on the National Youth Assistance program.

But we were happy. We were a family. Even though we lived on what today would be considered a poverty-level income, we didn't think of ourselves as poor. At the close of each Sunday dinner we sang the doxology "Now Blessed be Jehovah God, the God of Israel" and lingered at the table to talk with the guests—many times missionaries—who had joined us for the meal. We children all graduated from college, and most of us pursued service-oriented careers.

When my mother died at eighty-two, my youngest brother sang her favorite hymn, "Nearer, Still Nearer," at her funeral. His lovely tenor voice broke into sobs in the middle of the song. A stroke had left our mother, who had worked hard to give us the barest necessities, unable to recognize us in her last years. She taught us to be both frugal and generous. She would walk a mile to pay a bill to save a three-cent stamp. We didn't grow up with a lot of possessions, but we were rich in love, in solid virtues, and in "the one thing needful to know to live and die happily" (from the Heidelberg Catechism)—faith in Jesus Christ and the determination to do his will.

Creature comforts are wonderful—a hot bath, a large rose garden, a manicured yard, chic clothing, nice furniture, a comfortable mattress, music, books. But when you hike up into the mountains, you can put everything you need in a twenty-pound pack. And you can marvel at God's creation just as well sitting on a sleeping bag eating a plate of camp food as you could if you were sitting in a limousine with a banquet spread before you and the key to a resort hotel room in your pocket.

We should thank God for our abundance and learn to share it in a stewardly way. We can enjoy our fine homes with their TVs, CD players, and VCRs. But many have found, through experiences of deprivation, that those are not the important things. Witness the victims of earthquakes, hurricanes, and fire storms as they walk by the empty shells where their homes once stood. Naturally they weep for what they had, but many say, "We have each other. That's all that really matters," or "God will take care of us."

When life, that fragile beginning of our eternity, turns to death for each of us in one brief moment, we will take nothing with us. Nothing but the bare necessity—our faith in Jesus Christ our Savior. Nothing else will matter.

You provide for me abundantly, Father, and you shower me with blessings every day. But there are many who do not have the bare necessities of life. Help me to be diligent in helping those who lack food, shelter, medical care, and the assurance of salvation in Jesus Christ. Amen.

What Is This Thing Called Love?

How priceless is your unfailing love!
—*Psalm 36:7*

"By this all men will know that you are my disciples,
if you love one another."
—*John 13:35*

I love you, O LORD, my strength.
—*Psalm 18:1*

"One of the tragedies of American life is that love is being defined by those who have experienced so little of it," an author wrote.

There's a lot of truth in that statement. Look at divorce statistics, physical and sexual abuse reports, the high proportion of babies born out of wedlock, the popularity of prostitution, and the filth put out by video and television producers. Yet when we register complaints against pornography, we are called puritans. When we are repulsed by TV programs that show unmarried couples living together and unashamedly rolling together between the sheets, we are called Victorian prudes. The rationale is that as long as you love someone, anything goes.

A brooding old Cole Porter tune asks the question,

> What is this thing called love?
> This funny thing called love?
> Just who can solve its mystery?
> Why should it make a fool of me?
> I saw you there one wonderful day.
> You took my heart and threw it away.
> That's why I ask the Lord in heaven above,
> What is this thing called love?

Well, what is it? Can you define it without getting mushy or overly philosophical? I once asked a Bible class of thirty women to define it. I got thirty different answers.

Concepts like love and truth seem to defy definition because of their complexity. Perhaps our difficulty is that we are mortal; on this side of heaven the truth that God is love is hard to understand in its simplicity.

Many elements make up our definition of love—sizzling hormones, parent-child love, spousal love, friendship, devotion to one person, a loving God, care for others, romantic ballads, memories of past relationships, unselfishness, self-sacrifice, tenderness, fondness, affection, sexual attraction. All this, and we still haven't put our finger on the elusive quality that best describes love. The word *love* appears hundreds of times in the Bible. Adjectives that describe it include unfailing, faithful, eternal, compassionate, long-suffering, constant, merciful, and great.

Love is a score of zero in tennis. For many people that's also true in the game of life. A well-known actress said recently that marriage to her ex-husband, an actor, was good for business. Success, which she would have achieved anyway, came earlier than if she had not been married to him. So it was a good business arrangement. Now she has moved on to a new husband.

One of my husband's colleagues once complained that his wife always whined, "Do you love me?" My husband simply replied, "Well, do you?" A perplexed and frustrated look came over the man's face as he blurted, "Well, I married her, didn't I?"

It's sad not to be loved, but it's sadder not to be able to love. In order to truly love, we need to first affirm that God is love. We love because God first loved us. In his fourth thesis, Martin Luther said, "God does not love us because we're valuable; but we are valuable because He loves us." From that premise, from our recognition of God's love for us, we can love God and others.

William Temple noted, "Love of God is the root; love of neighbor the fruit of the Tree of Life. Neither can exist without the other—the one the cause, the other the effect—and the order of the Two Great Commandments must not be inverted." 1 John 4:20 says, "If anyone says, 'I love God,' yet hates his brother, he is a liar."

Hate comes naturally, but love must be learned. God did not advise us to love or suggest that it's a nice thing to do. He commanded it. Love God. Love your neighbor as yourself. No room for negotiations there. I must admit it's a relief to know we can love others without actually liking them or approving of their actions. Perhaps that's why some divorced couples say they get along better as friends than as mates.

God is the example of love. God is love. The Father loved so much, so unselfishly, so compassionately that he gave his own Son to die for us, to take on our sin, to carry our filthy rags of guilt and shame.

I treasure these words from a familiar hymn:

> Teach me to love you as your angels love,
> one holy passion filling all my frame:
> the fullness of the heaven-descended Dove;
> my heart an altar, and your love the flame.

Only when this happens can human relationships start to have real meaning. Only then can anyone try to define love. Only then can we begin to love as God meant.

You loved me before I knew you, and you taught me that people will know I am your disciple by how much I love you and others. Teach me, Lord, to love you as I should. May all people everywhere learn that they can have true fulfillment only in the context of your perfect love. Amen.

Prescription for Mediocrity

"Be perfect, therefore, as your heavenly Father is perfect."
—*Matthew 5:48*

I have always felt uncomfortable with the song that goes, "Give me that old time religion; it's good enough for me." I suppose when people sing that song they sincerely mean that they hold to "the faith of the fathers" as opposed to many religions in which the gospel of Christ is watered down or ignored. The "fathers" were very religious and knew right from wrong. They knew what was best. The "old time religion" was solid, basic, biblical, and that's what these people want.

I appreciate that attitude. The basics of the Christian faith must remain unchanged. We need a tried and true religious foundation.

Yet often the "old time religion" the song speaks of was one of isolation—a fort for a beleaguered tribe unconcerned about those outside. It often ignored what the implications of an active, vibrant faith should be, what a Christian "world and life" mind-set is. For people today, following an "old time religion"—a religion of someone else, who lived at another time—does not always lead to personal faith. It can become religion without spirituality. Didn't the Pharisees, too, think they were following the "old time religion" when they emphasized the letter rather than the spirit of the law?

When I study church history and world history in general, I am often dismayed by and ashamed of what occurred in the name of Christianity. Self-serving, pietistic leaders commandeered events and manipulated people's thoughts; leaders made the church mirror their own image rather than God's; egotistical church members carved out their selfish niche in the religious community; communities were rent by petty schisms. So often throughout history, religious leaders were not at all spiritual.

I am thankful that much of church history is encouraging and exciting. The gospel did go forth. Souls were saved. Lives were changed. Many great leaders came forward to lead the church in growth and piety. They did not settle for mediocrity. We cannot underestimate the role of the church throughout history in redeeming the times, in keeping life human and sane, and in bringing the lost to Christ. The church's comfort, amid success and failure, is the statement Jesus made so many years ago:

"On this rock I will build my church, and the gates of Hades will not overcome it" (Matthew 16:18).

So what really is meant by "that old time religion"? In an imperfect world in which God still demands perfection, do we ever have the right to say that anything—our history, our beliefs, our church, our religion—is "good enough for me"? The phrase *good enough* is intrinsically comparative. If it's only good enough, then there must be something better to which we are not aspiring.

Here is a scenario many church members will recognize: you're in a committee meeting, grappling with how to improve your worship services or the perception others have of your church or your fellowship with visitors or your mission outreach—when you hear someone lackadaisically say, "If it isn't broken, don't fix it. If that's the way we've always done something, how can it be wrong?"

We're very eager to improve our bodies with exercise and a healthy diet. We want to improve ourselves mentally and emotionally by becoming educated, avoiding stress, and developing a sense of humor. Farmers continually seek to improve their crops and herds; businesses offer incentives for ideas that will increase their output; industries seek state-of-the-art equipment to attract new buyers.

In the church, however, ideas for making improvements—for enhancing community outreach and personal witnessing, for making worship more meaningful, or for producing contemporary statements of faith—are often viewed with suspicion. They are seen as the fruit of liberal minds and are rejected because "the way we do it now is okay." We're satisfied with the status quo. We've always done it this way. Let sleeping dogs lie. Don't rock the boat. Don't attack our complacency or make us think. We don't want a ride down the slippery slope.

Such an attitude is a prescription for mediocrity. Take one good-enough capsule per day with a large glass of self-satisfaction.

Some settle for "good enough" by arguing that we're only human. That is a cop-out. True, we are not to make changes simply because change is fashionable. But when I consider the writings of Paul, Thomas Aquinas, Thomas à Kempis, Hannah Whitall Smith, the Reformers, and others who struggled to know the will of God and to be better Christians, I'm struck not by the thought that they were attempting to be superhuman, but by their genuine desire to root out all evil in thoughts and deeds, to rise above the common and mundane, and to portray more of the virtues listed in the Beatitudes. They desired to examine their motives, purify their hearts, meditate more deeply, love God more wholeheartedly, and understand Christ more fully.

What if Martin Luther had been content with the faith of his father—a justification-by-works philosophy? What if John Bunyan had never felt a soul-struggle nor seen life as a hard pilgrimage toward heaven? What if Paul hadn't run the race and attained the prize, but was content to come trotting down the track after all other contestants had left with their ribbons? Paul constantly struggled with the reality of sin—of doing what he should not have done and not doing what he should have done. None of the true leaders of the church settled for mediocrity. They reached out for God. They wanted to be and do better. They strove for victory. They weren't satisfied with "good enough," with the mediocre. They wanted what God wanted—the best.

Lord, I want to do my best for you. Keep me from being complacent and easily satisfied with myself. May I not use my imperfect human nature as an excuse for mediocre performance or for not striving to go beyond what seems "good enough." Amen.

God's Gift of Music

---

*The priests took their positions, as did the Levites with
the LORD's musical instruments, which King David
had made for praising the LORD.*
—2 *Chronicles 7:6*

Several years ago I was sitting with my husband in the plush seats of
San Francisco's Opera House listening to an "open rehearsal" of the city's
symphony orchestra. We often attended these daytime rehearsals because
we found them not only more convenient, but cheaper and more interesting.

The rehearsals were always informal and intimate. Instrumentalists
wore casual clothing. We had seen Isaac Stern wearing sweatpants and
tennis shoes as he practiced with the orchestra and chatted with the audience. We had felt the keen intensity with which Andre Watts played the
piano. We'd heard famous vocalists and instrumentalists and had seen
several different conductors in action.

This time again, after a coffee and doughnut social, we listened to a
music commentator from a local university analyze the works to be
played—instruments used, unusual passages, rhythmic patterns, repetitive
themes and counter-themes. Then the rehearsal began.

Of all the open rehearsals we had attended, this was most memorable,
a special moment in my life. I don't recall which symphony was played,
but it was soothing and unspeakably beautiful; and it affected me in a
mystical way that almost defies description.

My eyes were closed. As the music penetrated my soul, everything
else—the lovely hall, the people around me, my own thoughts and concerns—disappeared. I seemed to soar higher and higher, into the very
presence of God. It was a kind of out-of-body experience, and I had never
felt such profound peace. I wanted to stay there at the gates of heaven,
imbibing the sweetness and tranquility of the moment.

The mood was suddenly shattered by the sound of loud applause. I
seemed to fall with a thump back in my seat. A sense of sadness and depression came over me. I was not taking hallucinogenic drugs, nor was I
unhappy with life and eager for a way out. I only recall not wanting to

leave that high point because it seemed a foretaste of heaven. Had God arranged that moment for me?

I recall another time when, walking quietly in the Canterbury Cathedral in England, I heard a boys' choir singing "He watching over Israel" from Mendelssohn's *Elijah*. The angelic voices echoed through the long, high-ceilinged cathedral, where only a few others had gathered. Again it was a bit of heaven on earth—like standing on holy ground.

Today, all kinds of sounds are considered music—primal beats, cacophony, atonalism, screams and bestial groans, country, gospel, rap, operatic arias, sweet blues, soul, sentimental jazz, pipe organs, and church bells. Whether inspired by God or the devil, these sounds affect people in many different ways. Music has that ability. It can enhance and ennoble our lives. It can make us want to dance and sing. But it can also bring out evil desires and base thoughts. It can dishonor God and make idiots of people. And it can ascend to God—the author of music—as sweet and glorious praise.

The Bible and the poets of old describe music as harmonious, uplifting, inspiring, and calming—music that produces dancing as well as meditation. All nature sings, for creation itself is the music of the spheres—a symphony in six movements. Sir Thomas Browne once said, "Music strikes me as a profound contemplation of the First Composer." The poet Henry Wadsworth Longfellow wrote,

> And the night shall be filled with music,
> And the cares that infest the day
> Shall fold their tents like the Arabs,
> And as silently steal away.

The playwright William Congreve expressed the appeal of music powerfully when he said,

> Music hath charms to soothe the savage beast,
> To soften rocks,
> Or bend a knotted oak.

Of all the fine arts, music has most succeeded in retaining a sense of dignity and humanity in a world often perverted by its own history and lack of sound judgment.

Music has the power to conjure up deep-seated memories, both good and bad. Many of the songs of World War II still deeply affect me. They remind me of blackouts, rationing, the Coast Guard ensign who became my husband, the horror of Pearl Harbor and the concentration camps, and the men I knew who died in the war. Crossing the English Channel from France some years ago, I felt tears running down my cheeks as we neared shore. The words "There'll be bluebirds over the white cliffs of Dover" came to mind. Similarly, many hymns bring back memories of childhood and provide inspiration, joy, and comfort for the present.

Wordsworth spoke of "the still, sad music of humanity." Indeed, much of our music expresses sadness—songs of the slaves in the South, rhythm and blues, funeral music, and classical works such as Giuseppe Verdi's *Requiem Mass*. The exiles in Babylon hung their harps on trees as the wind coaxed strange sounds from the strings. "Our captors demand a song of us," they cried. "How can we sing the songs of Zion in a foreign land?" In the 1960s, the song "Blowin' In the Wind" communicated the detachment some felt from a society they felt was out of joint.

In a broader sense, the sad music of humanity is the discordant litany of a world gone mad, the groaning dirges that announce our inhumanity to others, the awful tinkling of the broken mirrors that were meant to image the great conductor of the universe.

When this world ends and time dissolves into eternity, one of the blessings we can look forward to is joining in the music of heaven—sweet, harmonious, and indescribably beautiful—God's eternal symphony for the redeemed.

Lord, thank you for music and the effect it has on my soul.
I look forward to the music of heaven—to angel's songs
and to the magnificent chorus of the redeemed singing,
"Worthy is the Lamb!" Amen.

House Hunting

"In my Father's house are many rooms."
—John 14:2

I like to have breakfast at my kitchen table, overlooking a wide expanse of lawn and flowers. Along the length of the south side of my home is a covered patio raised two steps above ground level. The sheltered havens created beneath the roof's cross-beams seem to attract birds. They flit in and out and build nests from lawn clippings and twigs they find on the compost pile.

One spring morning as I sipped tea and read the newspaper, I noticed four or five birds vying for the same spot. They zoomed in, knocked each other around, and swooped down again from higher positions, creating a dizzying flurry of activity. I knew that in a few weeks all the arguing would be over and about twenty small nests would occupy the sheltered areas. Each area would be marked as the private property of a lucky sparrow couple. I knew, too, that each day I'd be sweeping up the strings and twigs that missed the mark in the nest-building process.

House hunting is a universal activity for all earth's creatures. The homeless of the world wander streets and alleys looking for cardboard or metal pieces from which to fashion a shelter from the cold. They sleep under bridges or sit on grates that carry warm air up from the belly of the earth. Immigrants crowd ten to a room and feel thankful for a floor and a thin blanket. In countries all over the world, children, parents, babies, and the elderly sleep on the ground by night and walk the streets by day— nomads in search of food and a dwelling place. Their feet are swollen; their bodies crave medicine; their spirits seek rejuvenation.

Animals scurry around to find holes, burrows, caves, and hidden vegetation in which to rest. Insects seek shelter in crevices in walls, the bottoms of flowerpots, and even rugs and clothes. Often stray puppies can find a loving home more easily than homeless people.

As I read the real estate section of the paper, I noted with sadness the advertisements for new homes being built on prime farm land in our rich agricultural valley. "A buyer's market," the ads proclaimed. On Sundays, these new housing areas are full of house hunters—many from the San Francisco Bay area—looking for cheaper homes. Some parts of our valley have the best soils in the world. A soil expert by profession, my husband could often identify a soil type by just looking at it and feeling it with his fingers. He decried the greed of developers in buying land that God obviously had placed here for agricultural use.

Of course, houses have to be built, especially in California, the land of sunshine and opportunity, to which out-of-staters and immigrants beat a relentless path. But there are vast areas not viable for agriculture where builders could go. Since we are caretakers of the land, we have a sacred trust to use it in the very best way.

I feel increasingly uncomfortable in my large, air-conditioned home. If dozens of refugees occupied it, I can imagine they would think they'd found heaven at last. A single mother with several children might be overjoyed to live in just one of my rooms. Though my home is often filled with grandchildren or guests, I wonder what I could do for those who need a good meal and a night's sleep. God provides us with earthly dwellings; they are a trust to be used for God's glory.

Think of Jesus' words in Matthew 8:20, where he challenged the disciples to a fuller commitment to him: "Foxes have holes and birds of the air have nests, but the Son of Man has no place to lay his head." Jesus, the King, didn't have a home of his own once he left his parents' protection. Nor was he concerned with having a home on earth. He was constantly pointing his followers to a heavenly home. He said there was lots of room in his Father's house, and he was going on ahead to prepare a mansion for his people.

Earthly house hunting consumes a lot of time and can lead to a large financial commitment, but finding a *permanent* home takes an even greater commitment. Yet a heavenly home with all its lovely rooms is free. No escrow worries. No mortgage payments. No investment in furniture. No termites, moths, or rust. No expensive repairs. No threat of eviction. Our only indebtedness is to Jesus, who provided the mansion for us. Think about house hunting for a permanent home. The fringe benefits are fantastic.

Thank you, Father, for the home you have given me.
Lead me to opportunities to share it with others. Most of all,
I praise you for providing a home in heaven where I can
live forever in fellowship with you. Prepare me for
that blessed day. Amen.

Daffodils in the Bathtub

He has made everything beautiful in its time.
—Ecclesiastes 3:11

If you are traveling in California in the springtime, there's a delightful spot in the historic Mother Lode country that you must see. To reach the area, you take the "forty-niners'" route part of the way, past tall-grassed pastureland bounded by old picket or barbed-wire fences. All of nature is alive. Little lambs rise on shaky feet and nuzzle up to their warm mother for nourishment. Bright orange poppies, purple lupines, butter-yellow mustard plants, and other native wildflowers dazzle the eyes.

Rounding a bend in the road, you suddenly see it. Daffodil Hill. Visited by thousands of people each year, the hill is a gorgeous panorama of yellow and white—the love gift of a family that opens its gardens to all who love flowers. The setting is reminiscent of a Wordsworth poem describing a similar scene in England's Lake Country.

On the hill, paths wind through giant flower patches. Freshly-covered picnic tables stand on the lower end of the hill. Peacocks spread their colorful feathers. Potted hyacinths, tulips, and daffodils are spread randomly throughout the gardens. I'm always fascinated by the variety of containers in which these flowers are planted—watering cans, washtubs, ancient washing machines with wringers removed, tin cans, cracked crockery, bent-up pails, and old water heaters cut in half lengthwise.

One especially draws my attention—a bathtub full of daffodils. Who would think of placing a cracked old tub on a manicured lawn and planting it full of flowers? But there it sits—a very old tub with claw-shaped feet, chock full of the long-stemmed beauties, weeds growing comfortably around it. In a different location, the tub would look tacky and out of place. But in this untamed, natural setting, it makes a charming display.

So what makes something or someone beautiful? Why does my granddaughter bring me a dandelion and say, "I picked the most beautiful flower in your garden," when I have almost a hundred rose bushes to pick from?

Beauty has been defined as "the subjective appreciation of objective qualities in what we see and hear." This is similar to the familiar saying, Beauty is in the eye of the beholder. To an artist, beauty is often found in expression—like the face of a mother gazing into the eyes of her newborn child. Men and women look at the human body with different ideas of what makes a person beautiful. Perhaps our perceptions of beauty depend on what we are looking for. A father might call his raggedy-haired, runny-nosed daughter beautiful. He knows of her sweet nature and loving disposition. He knows how she looks when she's lying freshly-bathed in her little bed. He knows she is his own.

Is everyone moved by beauty? Looking at the lovely surroundings in Berchtesgaden, Germany, where Hitler had his retreat, someone remarked that the man must have had some good in him to have picked such a beautiful spot. Surely God's common grace extends to all; we all bear God's image regardless of our attitude toward God. Does the murderer gazing out of his cell window feel something stir in him when the scent of lilacs reaches his nostrils? Can the blind feel beauty in the velvety petals of a rose, in the creases of a loved one's face, in the aroma of a favorite food? Do they perhaps "see" more beauty than sighted people?

In one sense, we make and find our own beauty, but in the deepest sense, we know that God is the author of all beauty. Thomas Aquinas noted that "the being of all things is derived from the Divine Beauty." Beauty, in its truest sense, is more than an aesthetic activity, a mental and spiritual experience, or a physical fact. It comes from God; it is an attribute of God's being.

In Matthew 26:10, Jesus rebuked the disciples for rumbling about the perfume a woman had "wasted" on him. He said she had done a beautiful thing and her deed would be told in memory of her wherever the gospel was preached around the world. Actions can be beautiful—a man jumping in the water to save a child but losing his own life; a child leading an elderly person across the street; a mother denying herself pretty clothes in order to dress her children well; the serene departure of a loved one to heaven; the Son of God hanging on a cross to take away our sins.

Earthly beauty is temporal. Flowers fade. Winter strips trees of their leaves. Beautiful men and women die. Natural disasters turn lovely things into nightmarish horrors. Bombs wipe out lovely cities. Moth and rust corrupt. Valuable artwork is destroyed by fire. Golden cities of old are buried beneath new civilizations. If we insist on defining beauty in terms of the physical, we are doomed to great disappointment. There will be nothing left but dust and ashes.

The footnote to Ecclesiastes 3:11 in the NIV Study Bible says, "God's beautiful but tantalizing world is too big for us, yet its satisfactions are too small. Since we were made for eternity, the things of time cannot fully and permanently satisfy." Beauty is subjective, fleeting, changing, imperfect. But in the new heaven and earth, every sound, every sight, every deed, every glorified body, will be beautiful forever.

Meanwhile, I'd like to grow in sanctification and mirror more and more the beauty of Jesus. And I'd like to keep going to the foothills to see the daffodils in the bathtub—at least until I get appointed to the grounds committee in heaven and can experience immortal beauty—pure, unmarred, and fadeless.

You created a spectacular world, Lord, and commanded us to care for it. Bless the efforts of those who try to beautify the earth. May my concept of beauty always be defined by the beauty in you, and may I reflect it in the way I live. Amen.

Peter People

Then Peter remembered the word Jesus had spoken. . . .
And he broke down and wept.
—Mark 14:72

"I tell you that you are Peter, and on this rock
I will build my church."
—Matthew 16:18

Before I became better acquainted with him, I had never considered Simon Peter one of my favorite Bible characters. I had always been attracted to people like Job, Daniel, and Luke—sturdy, purposeful, obedient characters. I felt a love-hate relationship with the "super woman" described in Proverbs. I knew Solomon was very wise, but I found his sexual appetite perplexing—really, seven hundred wives? And I loved David's poetry, but the Bathsheba affair always bothered me. If David lived today, he would receive a long prison term for ordering Bathsheba's husband killed so he could have her.

And then there was Simon Peter. Bold. Impulsive. Rough. Cocksure. I could hear the swarthy, dark-bearded man shouting coarsely to the fishermen in surrounding boats. I could see him, dirty and sweaty, as he pulled the nets in for the night after trying to walk on water to meet Jesus. I could picture him sitting with the two sons of Zebedee in the garden of Gethsemene the night Jesus went off to pray. Jesus had asked the men to stay awake, but every time he came back, he found them asleep. Parents stay up with sick children all night. Couldn't Peter, the disciple who promised he'd stick by Jesus, honor the Lord's request and keep his eyes open for one measly hour?

Simon Peter, the impulsive one, pulling out a sword and cutting off a man's ear. You could hardly call that sanctified problem-solving. And what about his word of honor? One moment he said he would lay down his life for Jesus, and the next moment he said he had never known him. No, Peter. No thanks. I'd stick to the humble, nonabrasive, quiet people of the Bible.

My negative feelings about Peter gradually changed, however, as I read further and met the real Peter. I had never studied his career and hadn't realized how much he changed. Yes, he had adamantly denied Jesus three times. But after the cock crowed, we are told, Jesus' eyes met Peter's. Peter knew what was in those eyes. And he went out the gate alone and wept bitterly. I could picture his strong body shaking convulsively as he leaned against the wall, slamming his fist until it bled. I could hear the large, salty tears hit the ground—tears of sorrow and deep repentance.

I read on. After Christ had risen, an angel told the women who had come to anoint Christ's body, "Go, tell his disciples and Peter" (Mark 16:7). And as all the other disciples stood in disbelief, Peter ran to the tomb.

Jesus' and Peter's eyes met a second time when Jesus asked the searing question, "Peter, do you love me?" This time the bravado was gone. This time Peter humbly submitted his love to the judgment of Jesus: "Lord, you know all things; you know that I love you" (John 21:17). Peter and Jesus were reconciled in that encounter. Later, Peter confidently affirmed that Jesus Christ was the Son of the living God, and he became, as Jesus had said, the rock upon which the church was built.

As I read the Acts of the Apostles and Peter's letters to the elect, I realized Jesus had transformed Peter from a rough, bumbling fisherman to a polished speaker who could stand boldly before the Sanhedrin and defend his healing of the sick in the name of the Lord. His passion for Christ emboldened him to preach with conviction, suffer imprisonment, and go back out to defend his Lord. He made good on his earlier brash statements of fidelity to Jesus when he died a martyr during the reign of Nero. God had taken what seemed to be undesirable characteristics and turned them into the qualities of a leader.

While studying the book of Mark, I sensed that the words "Go, tell his disciples and Peter" might just as well have read, "Go, tell the disciples and Ruth." I am a Peter person. I am not a "super saint," and even though I've been a follower all my life, I have denied Jesus many times in thought, word, and deed. When Jesus reached out to Peter, Peter felt the joy of reconciliation. When Jesus seeks me out, he brings me comfort, forgiveness, and acceptance. I have the same joy and assurance as Peter.

Every Christian has a one-on-one relationship with Christ. Christ comes to each of us, calls us by name, recognizes our failures, and initiates reconciliation. We have only to confess him as Lord. He then gives us forgiveness and acceptance.

Followers of Christ are Peter people. The Holy Spirit had to take us all—gems in the rough—and put us in the spiritual rock tumbler to grind off the jagged spots: our pride, arrogance, intolerance, unfaithfulness, self-satisfaction, and false piety.

For all Christians the cock has crowed, and if we have never felt the need to weep bitterly for our sins, perhaps we have not stood long enough at the cross. Everyone's eyes must meet those of Jesus. The look in his eyes will either condemn us or forgive us.

Jesus renamed Simon. He called him Peter—not for what Peter was, but for what he would become by the grace of God. Similarly, he calls us the redeemed because he takes us Simon people and makes us Peter people—builders of his church.

Lord, I've heard it, too—the crowing of the cock. Help me to stand up and be counted as your disciple even if I must suffer for it. Thank you for your forgiveness when I deny you in my thoughts and actions. Make me a Peter person, Lord, as I try to become more like you. Amen.

Corner on the Truth

*Now we see but a poor reflection as in a mirror; then we
shall see face to face. Now I know in part; then I shall
know fully, even as I am fully known.*
—*1 Corinthians 13:12-13*

When I was growing up, my siblings and I played basic games like
checkers, dominoes, and pick-up sticks. But one Christmas we received
the card game Pit. It was exciting, and we played it with enthusiasm and
passion.

Pit was our introduction to the world of buying, selling, and trading. It
involved grain commodities such as oats, rye, wheat, and corn. The object
was to get a corner on the market—to get a all the cards in a set. It was a
noisy game, with each player trying to persuade the others to make trades
and trying to make himself heard above the others. Getting a corner on
the market was the all-important and all-consuming purpose.

My own children played Pit a few decades later and seemed to have as
much of a noisy good time with it as their uncles, aunts, and I had. The
play could be intense, but it was only an innocent game.

There is a version of that game, however, that is played in political, social, and religious circles. It is played by leaders and members of churches,
groups, and organizations. This game is called Corner on the Truth. It
isn't innocent. It is a sinful, unbiblical, and harmful attempt to gain control and power over the minds and souls of men and women. Those playing the game do it so subtly that others need not be naive to fall for it.

Perceiving yourself or your group as having a corner on the truth is
spiritual arrogance. It often leads to the unjust condemnation, persecution, and even death of those who oppose it. It is difficult to counteract
because the "truth-holders" regularly invoke the name of God and quote
the Bible as they impose guilt and a sense of spiritual inferiority on those
who disagree with them. These truth-holders also claim a corner on God,
saying God speaks to them and tells them things the rest don't know.

The mass suicides of several cult groups in recent years are examples of
what can happen when one person or group claims a corner on the truth.
Leaders of these groups subtly lure people into their power trap. History
is full of examples of kings, heads of state, even entire countries that im-

posed their beliefs on the masses. Ironically, the truth is not the real concern; it is only an excuse to gain power and authority.

I am not talking about sincere Christians who hold to what are generally considered the basic tenets of biblical faith—the fall, the virgin birth, God's offer of salvation, Christ's sacrifice, justification by faith, and the infallibility of Scripture. My concern is with those who see everything in black and white. For them there is no looking through a glass darkly. They see everything in perfect clarity. Gray areas exist only in the minds of so-called liberals. These truth-holders are the people who falsely persecuted Galileo for his beliefs about the earth and the planets. They are the people in my denomination's history who denounced the radio as a "tool of the devil" and the use of individual communion cups as a deviation from the teachings of Scripture.

People with a corner on the truth may outshout everyone else, but they do not want to discuss issues (for example, women being "allowed" to vote or hold offices in the church) because, they say, "there is nothing to discuss." Just read your Bible, they say. Homosexuals are all going to hell. Many of society's ills are a result of women's insistence on taking jobs and leaving the kitchen, where they were meant to be. Psychologists and psychiatrists are completely unnecessary, because people would never have depression if they stayed close to God. The word "self-esteem" comes straight from the vocabulary of the humanists. On and on they go.

Paul is right when he says we must not be "blown here and there by every wind of teaching" (Eph. 4:14). But it is also true that we are sinful and fallible. We do not have all the answers. Human confessions and interpretations can be changed as we gain new insights in studying the original biblical texts or as we find some long-held interpretations erroneous because of faulty translations. When Paul said, "Listen, I tell you a mystery" (1 Cor. 15:51), he was talking about a truth formerly not understood but now revealed.

When cultists brainwash adherents to the point that they will die for the cause; when people leave a church because they and they alone are right; when believers will not fellowship with one another because they disagree on issues not essential to salvation; and when church councils impose their ideas on matters which rightfully belong to the conscience of individual believers—they all have declared themselves authorities on truth and have condemned those who believe or interpret differently.

In the beautifully poetic passages of Job 37 and following, God challenges Job's complaints with the words, "Who is this that darkens my counsel without knowledge?" (Job 38:2). With this question and others,

God illustrates our limited comprehension. It's good to read this passage when we are tempted to claim special dispensation from God, or when our puffed-up egos would have us claim a corner on the truth. The fact that there are many Christian denominations shows that even the most educated theologians cannot agree.

Each person, it seems to me, should find a set of beliefs that he or she feels most nearly embodies the truths of Scripture and then serve God humbly, waiting for the day when no darkened glass separates us from the face of God. Then no one will have a corner on the truth. Everyone in the new heaven and earth will have a full set of winning cards.

Lord, keep me from the arrogance of considering myself an authority on your revelation in nature and in the Bible. Humble me when I insist on my interpretation in the "gray areas" of society and the church, but help me to proclaim boldly that you are the way, the truth, and the life. Amen.

Loosen Up!

*I have become all things to all men so that by all
possible means I might save some.*
—*1 Corinthians 9:22*

Over the years, we have had a number of guests from foreign countries
in our home, but one couple stands out because of how little they
attempted to adjust to unfamiliar foods, mores, or points of view. They
expected to be served foods they were used to. They looked with suspicion and disdain on some of our meals. They wanted to do everything on
their own schedule. They were openly critical of many American customs, of America's political and military policies, and even of our method
of eating a sandwich.

I bought special foods for them. I made giant pots of coffee (which I
don't drink) and tried to find the kind of pillows they used back home.
They didn't want to see local attractions because nothing could match the
beauties in their own country. They sat at the table when they thought it
was time to eat, whether the food was ready or not. I was relieved when
the week-long visit was over. I had to do all the adjusting and still didn't
feel as though my guests were satisfied. I felt like an unappreciated
innkeeper.

Anyone who has done some traveling knows that we must be willing to
adjust to different lifestyles and broad-minded enough to realize that
there are many ways to live, varying opinions to consider, different ways
to dress, and a number of customs to observe out of courtesy to our hosts.
In these areas of life no one way should be declared right or best.

In our family travels to Europe, our children were at first inflexible;
they even made fun of some of the things they saw and ate. But soon,
with patient talks and anecdotes from their father, they learned to appreciate different cultures and conditions and to enjoy the challenge of learning about new people and foods.

Their father told them about the time he was in a foxhole in the South
Pacific during World War II with a wealthy, spoiled, big-city serviceman.
The man spent the night screaming at insects and berating his government for making him live in such awful conditions. The men in foxholes
around him were awakened regularly by the man's yelling and ranting.

Finally they dug the complainer a hole far away from them and dumped him in it. Then they all went back to sleep. They knew how to loosen up and adjust to their circumstances.

Sometimes in our travels, we witnessed what is meant by "the Ugly American." These tourists were demanding and intolerant. They complained about the outmoded plumbing, the unripe fruit, the straight-backed pews in old churches, English meals, hamburgers made from ham, high prices, waiting in lines, late airplanes, and rooms without air-conditioning or private baths. They were so inflexible, so steeped in their own way of doing things, that criticism was their natural response. They should have stayed home.

Intolerant people are unyielding, incapable of change, persistent, stubborn, and resistant to persuasion or softening influences. Their way is the only way. They refuse to reconsider long-held views and positions. They fail to realize that unfamiliar experiences can be fascinating and broadening.

There is in all of us a fear of the unknown, an apprehension about unfamiliar people, cultures, and philosophies. We are comfortable with those who think and act as we do. We become inflexible, however, when we refuse to loosen up and roll with the punches. We are inflexible if we cannot tolerate discussion of a viewpoint with which we disagree; if we are threatened by cultural diversity—by people who speak another language and have customs we think odd or foolish.

Such inflexibility often carries over into our religious life. It carries over into our perceptions of those who believe differently from us or who have a history of evildoing that we cannot tolerate. Our witness of God's love is seriously hampered when we demand conformity in lifestyle, customs, and attitudes.

In a March 15, 1993, *Time* magazine article, Lance Morrow analyzed the behavior of cultists. He said, "Religion is sometimes a fortress for the beleaguered tribe in a new world disorder . . . who go from intelligent tolerance on the one hand toward irrational religious tribalism on the other." He described cultists as "a group sealed away in paranoia—an act of cultural symbolism framed in religious context." Church people sometimes fit that description, too, even though they would never describe themselves as cultists.

We do well to remember that tolerance is not synonymous with compromise. Nor should tolerance suggest begrudgingly putting up with someone or something. Paul did not use that terminology. He said he had become all things to all people in the hopes of saving some. The footnote in my Bible says, "Paul accommodated himself to Gentile culture when it did not violate his allegiance to Christ." Because of his love for the Corinthians, he forfeited many of his rights. He sacrificed practices that he felt were consistent with his faith when they hindered the weaker members. He curtailed his social and religious privileges in dealing with some people in order to bring them to Christ. He learned to "hang loose," to be flexible, not uptight.

Christians who know they are redeemed only by the grace of God will not be intimidated or threatened by what some might consider strange, dangerous, unacceptable, or unworthy people. We may not decide who is "saint material." Jesus sought out prostitutes, thieves, tax collectors, and other "undesirables." Paul was accepting and seeker-friendly. He adjusted to his surroundings and made people comfortable as he sought to win them.

There is a product for stiff, unbending joints called Flex-All. Perhaps we who bear the name Christian, who claim to want to bring the world to a saving knowledge of Jesus Christ, need a spiritual Flex-All to help us loosen up for the unchurched. God would be thrilled to see ex-drug addicts, ex-people abusers, ex-streetwalkers, saintly grandmas, members steeped in the creeds and confessions, church leaders, ethnic minorities, the poor, and the rich all loving and accepting one another as fellow image-bearers of Christ.

Father, if you can put up with all my faults and idiosyncrasies, surely I can adjust to those who think or live differently than I. Teach me how to be all things to all people for the sake of the gospel and to love and show respect to all people, for they were created in your perfect image. Amen.

Like a Little Child

"Whoever humbles himself like this child is the greatest in the kingdom of heaven."
—Matthew 18:4

He sat pensively, chin cupped in his sturdy hands, elbows resting on my kitchen table. Though only eight years old, my oldest grandson was already a big help to me in taking care of my large garden. We had worked for three hours trimming bushes and cleaning up the brush. Now we sat facing each other, chatting over our cold drinks and cookies.

Suddenly he stopped drinking, and as his large brown eyes met mine he asked, "Grandma, would you want to live to be one hundred years old?" I answered quickly, "No, Peter, too many things go wrong with the body as you get older—your senses dim, bones can break, hair and teeth fall out, your mind can get fuzzy . . ." He interrupted my monologue with his own answer: "I wouldn't either, Grandma; I don't want to wait that long to see Jesus."

We talked then about heaven, and I wondered aloud how I would find all the people with whom I want to have a reunion when I get there. Peter's response was spontaneous and natural. "No problem, Grandma," he said with complete assurance. "When you die, a huge elevator takes you right up to the gate, and Jesus will be standing there with a big microphone. When he sees you he'll say, 'H-e-e-e-ere's Ruth,' and Grandpa, Uncle Dan, and all your family and friends will be there just like that. Isn't that neat?"

A few weeks later, Peter's mom got resistance from her children as she tried to determine who was to blame for a misdeed. She told Peter and his sister, "One of you knows who did it and won't tell, but you know that God knows exactly who is at fault." Five-year-old Katie stared hard into her mom's eyes and asked, finally, "Well, is he telling you?"

What is it about a child's faith that is so different from an adult's that it caused Jesus to rebuke his disciples and call a little child to stand among them? While the disciples argued over who was the greatest in the kingdom, Jesus said, "I tell you the truth, unless you change and become like little children, you will never enter the kingdom of heaven. Therefore, whoever humbles himself like this little child is the greatest in the kingdom of heaven."

The words smack us between the eyes. A child? Greatest in the kingdom? What does a child know about doctrines, the attributes of God, the mysteries of the incarnation? Have kids ever heard about regeneration, advent, justification by faith, inerrancy, or the "holy catholic church"?

Is knowledge irrelevant in our quest for the riches of the kingdom and our place in it? I don't think so. But it is irrelevant in the context of this meeting of the disciples and the child. Jesus was talking about the heart and character of a child—unpretentious, trusting, believing. Jesus said that those who humble themselves as a little child are the greatest in the kingdom.

True, children ask lots of questions. God gave them minds with which to think and reason. They are curious and want answers. What makes their faith so exemplary for adults, however, is that with all the questions they have, they always seem to have the assurance that there are answers and that God can do anything. They don't ask cynically. Their imaginations can fill in the blanks. Nothing is impossible.

Like a child, I also know God can do anything, but all kinds of theological concerns, physical laws, and past experiences invade my thoughts. An elevator all the way to heaven? Impossible. God announcing me, Johnny Carson-style? How ridiculous! God telling a mother which child is guilty? Dream on. God's got more important things to think about. God needing a microphone? How naive!

And yet, why was my answer to Peter's question about living to one hundred conditioned by physical aspects, while Peter's was spiritual—"I don't want to wait that long to see Jesus"? Why did Katie think her mom had a hot line to God? Was it maybe because Katie has one? Or was she just an innocent and unschooled child who hears, believes, and makes her own world fit in with this fantastic God who can do anything? Of course, the explanations children give are often simplistic and farfetched, even a little silly. Jesus isn't telling us to *think* the way children do, with their limited understanding and fairy-tale conclusions. He is telling us to *be* the way children are.

Have we as adults become a bit doubting, skeptical, lacking in complete trust? Do we as disciples of Christ sometimes have too sophisticated a faith commitment, a superior feeling about the quality of our spirituality? Or do the harsh experiences of life leave us distrustful of a God who seems to be absent when we cry out against injustices and hurts? Do we lack the humility that Jesus and the little child both exemplified?

We are told not to be childish. We are to put away childish things. But we are to be childlike. In the eyes of God we are all children—God's adopted ones. 1 John 3:1 says, "How great is the love the Father has lavished on us, that we should be called children of God! And that is what we are!"

Is the father-child relationship too humbling as we walk across the stage of life performing our successful, sophisticated, spiritual, sanctified roles? Jesus said that his disciples—and that's what we claim to be—had to change and become like little children in order to be great in the kingdom. I need that reminder. How peaceful and exciting it would be to see Jesus and life and heaven through the eyes of a child again.

Lord, help me to see you and your kingdom through the eyes of a child. Give me a faith that does not limit your greatness or doubt your ability to make an elevator climb heavenward. May I be as humble, unpretentious, and trusting as one of your little ones. Amen.